Unleashed

A Play

John Godber

A SAMUEL FRENCH ACTING EDITION

SAMUEL FRENCH

FOUNDED 1830

SAMUELFRENCH-LONDON.CO.UK
SAMUELFRENCH.COM

ISBN 978-0-573-01927-2

www.samuelfrench-london.co.uk

www.samuelfrench.com

UNLEASHED

This version first performed by the Hull Truck Theatre
Company at the Bloomsbury Theatre, London, on 18th
October 1999, with the following cast:

Mick	Nick Lane
Bob	Bill Ilkley
Gary	Zach Lee
Natasha	Joanne Jolly
Tish	Rebecca Clay

Directed by **John Godber**
Designed by **Pip Leckonby**

CHARACTERS

Amsterdam: The Sex Industry

Kev, sharp, keen; fronts a porn club, young
Tom, thick, slow, aggressive; fronts a porn club, middle-aged
Mick, ex art student; cleans up after the show, late 20s
Natasha, Czech prostitute; dumb but sexy, young
Tish, German prostitute, aggressive, desperate, late 30s

England: Domesticity

Dennis, mild-mannered office worker, middle-aged
Anabelle, fussy, kind housewife, middle-aged
Jenny, their raucous, soon-to-be law student daughter, young

The Office Men

Bob, sharp, sensitive, football-mad office type, early 40s
Gary, office worker, over-excitable, young

The play is set outside a live sex show in Amsterdam. The sex show is flanked by the two prostitutes; Natasha and Tish. Mick the Narrator plays Dennis, Kev plays Gary, Tom plays Bob, Natasha plays Jenny, and Tish plays Anabelle.

The sense of place outside the sex show is real, and so is the story within the story, which Mick is narrating. The sex industry is an illusion, thus is the story-telling device.

ACT I

The stage depicts an area of the red light district of Amsterdam. It should feel seedy and dangerous. A couple of windows—where prostitutes trade, the opening of a live sex club, and the facility for multi locations should be afforded by the set

As the audience enter, two prostitutes, Natasha, a young Czech, and Tish, an older German, sit in their windows

Music: Joan Osborne's One of Us

Two wide-boy porn hawkers, Tom (lugubrious and slow) and Kev (sharp and alert), mingle amongst the audience. They attempt to get the audience in to see the Live Sex Show. *They call out quickly "Live sex show, sucky licky show"; their delivery should be deadpan and matter of fact*

As they hawk their wares, Mick, a Yorkshire youth in his late 20s, wanders on to the stage. He is dressed in casual clothes. He picks up a mobile bucket and a mop, inspects a cubicle on stage, and commences to mop

Music fades

Tom and Kev move towards the stage and front up the porn club. Mick mops

Mick Dirty bastards!
Kev Sucky, licky show!
Tom Live show!
Kev Live sex show!
Mick (*mopping*) What have they been playing at in there? Somebody's thrown up!
Kev Sucky, licky show!

Mick mops, Tom and Kev try and keep warm

Tom Who's on at the moment, then?
Kev Sonia.
Tom Who's that, then?

Mick (*mopping*) Dirty bastards!

Kev Sonia, the German.

Tom Which one is she, then?

Kev She does that candle act. Have you seen it?

Mick Half of Europe have seen it!

Tom It's rubbish.

Kev She's a German, does a candle act. She does that thing with a candle, have you not seen it?

Tom It's rubbish, man!

Kev It's good.

Tom Is it hell!

Kev She's good.

Tom Useless!

Kev We've got a new girl and all! She's Dutch, I think. A student!

Tom A student?

Mick I came here as a student.

Kev A law student?

Tom A law student!

Mick Came and stayed.

Tom She a lawyer, then?

Kev Going to be.

Tom What's she doing down here, then?

Kev Dunno!

Tom What's she doing down here if she's going to be a lawyer?

Kev Paying for college, I expect.

Tom Paying for college?

Mick (*mopping*) I was going to do Europe.

Kev That's what she's doing!

Mick Jumped on a ferry in Hull, but I only got as far as here!

Kev She's twenty-one!

Mick Came to study art!

Kev Marga they call her, she's a Dutch lass.

Tom Sucky, licky show!

Kev Live show!

Tom I never fancied college!

Kev No?

Tom I fancied studying law!

Kev You?

Tom Always fancied that. Live sucky show!

Kev Sucky show, this way!

Mick It was the Dutch masters that I came here for. Vermeer, and Frans Hals. Then I discovered Van Gogh and realized art is a matter of perception.

Tom What's he on about?

Kev Art?
Mick It's a matter of perception!
Kev This is not art.
Mick Well, it's not Van Gogh!
Tom What is art anyway?
Kev Oh, don't start!
Tom Is it a bowl of flowers or some squiggles on a page?
Kev Live sex show this way!
Mick Philistines!

A beat. Mick mops

Tom I'd got this girl back to my apartment once...
Kev When?
Tom Once.
Kev Who was this, then?
Tom All she wanted to do was talk about art...
Kev Who was this, then?
Tom I thought I was well in, but...
Kev Who was this, then?
Tom She was just going on about Salvador Dali...
Kev Who was this, then?
Tom Talia!
Kev From the Cassa Rossa?
Tom She does a lesbo show!
Mick It's a good show!
Kev She a les?
Tom No.
Kev You took a les back to your place and talked about art?
Tom She's not a les.
Kev She does a lesbo show!
Tom She does a lesbo show, but she's not a les! She's an actress or sommat!
Kev She's a junkie, i'n't she?
Mick That's how I ended up in here. I was stoned on space cake and somebody asked if I wanted to help out.
Tom Just rabbiting on about Dali.
Kev She worked that sex shop near the Crowne Plaza.
Mick It was a way to see all the acts at first. Now I don't watch the acts, I watch the punters.
Tom Took her back to my apartment once.
Mick Jan asked, had I any experience of selling things? I said I once worked on a coconut shy at Hull fair!
Tom Off her head!

Kev Did you shag her?
Tom Just rabbiting on about concepts.
Kev Off her head?
Tom I thought, sod that, and I went to bed.

A beat

Mick I saw three old women in one of these booths yesterday. Can you believe that? How the hell do you get three women in one of them cubicles? They should tell Norris McWhirter about that!
Kev Have you seen Zena's act?
Tom Which one's she, then?
Kev Blond. Tall, big tits.
Tom Which act is that, then?
Kev It's her and them two blokes!
Tom Her and two blokes?
Kev It's not bad!
Tom Isn't it?
Kev It's not a bad act.
Tom What is it, her and two blokes?
Kev Yes, it's her and them two big blokes. It's a good act, she puts a lot into it!
Tom Which is more than can be said for most of 'em!
Mick About a month ago I saw a bloke from home down here!
Kev Live sex show!
Mick I thought: what's he doing?
Tom That's Zena, then, is it?
Kev That's Zena!
Tom I'd heard her name but I didn't know which act…
Kev That's Zena, her and two blokes.
Mick I thought, I know him. It was Dennis Ashby, they used to live on our estate, and then they flitted.
Kev Yes, please, ladies!
Mick I thought: what's he up to? I mean, he came in here three times, and then he was hanging about waiting for Natasha and Tish!
Tom Is she married, then?
Kev Who?
Tom Zena?
Kev Not to those two!
Tom No?
Kev They're gay.
Mick That's what I do. I watch the punters, I start to fill in the gaps.
Tom Both gay, then?
Kev I think.

Mick I wonder what they get up to.

Tom and Kev eye someone who is walking past them down the street

Kev Yes, please, you like sexy girls?
Tom Arsehole!
Mick I started to think, what would his wife say?
Kev I might go in and watch Sonia!
Tom I thought you'd seen her?
Mick I began to wonder where he lives!
Kev I have, but it's a good act. I think she's got real talent. I could sit through it again.
Tom It's rubbish, it's boring. She just plays about with a candle, and then it disappears!
Kev Yes, it's a candle act. It's a good act.
Tom It's shite!
Kev It's not.
Tom It's absolutely fucking pointless, to me!
Kev Live show.
Tom Sucky fucky licky show!
Mick I began to wonder what he was like when he got home? Did he tell her that he'd been hanging about down here? I've got this whole scenario about Dennis. I can just see him arriving back with a bunch of tulips in one hand and a carrier bag full of shit souvenirs in the other...

Music: Knocking on Heaven's Door *performed by Ladysmith Black. Mick gets a raincoat and some glasses. He is handed a bunch of tulips and a carrier bag full of rubbishy souvenirs*

Tom and Kev exit

Mick now plays Dennis

Anabelle enters. She is fussy, prim and nervous, but a good soul

Music fades. Lights

Anabelle I thought you'd got lost!
Dennis Delayed two hours!
Anabelle Have you had a good time?
Dennis I had a bit of a struggle getting everything you wanted...
Anabelle Well, you needn't have bothered.
Dennis Well, you said you wanted something getting, so...

Anabelle No problem with the flowers?

Dennis That was the easy bit.

Anabelle They have such beautiful flowers, don't they?

Dennis And I managed to get some bulbs as well, there's a bulb market, I thought I'd get some. And I've got you some of that new perfume, Issey-something. They were going mad for it at the airport...

Anabelle Oh Dennis?

Dennis What's wrong?

Anabelle Well, it's the first time you've been away and actually brought me anything back!

Dennis It's not!

Anabelle Usually I'm lucky if I get a box of Quality Street.

Dennis Well, it's not every day I get a chance to...

Anabelle But it's daft, we're strapped for cash as it is!

Dennis Well, if I can't get you a bit of something...

Anabelle I'm not complaining, I'm just saying...

Dennis I can't do right, for doing wrong!

Anabelle Did Jenny ring you? I told her to, cheer you up a bit!

Dennis No, no, she rang, we had a right good chat. She seems fine.

Anabelle Well, I'd better get these into some water. They're lovely! I'll make you a coffee, shall I? (*She pecks Dennis on the cheek and takes the flowers and the bag of souvenirs*)

Dennis I think I might go away again; you get great treatment when you come back.

Anabelle Well, let me know in advance next time!

Anabelle exits

Mick (*to the audience*) I bet he works in one of those offices where everybody is trying like hell to be nice, but really they'd like to cut each other's throats!

Music: Boyce's Symphony No. 4 in F Major. Lights

Bob, a smart man in his early 40s, enters

He positions a computer table downstage. He sits at his desk and works on the computer

Gary enters. He is much younger, though appears tired

Bob sits at the computer screen and speaks casually over his shoulder. Music plays under the Lights

Gary Bob, lunch!

Bob Not today.

Gary Well, I'm nipping out to get a sandwhich, then I'm going to try to get my head down for five!

Bob Is she still not sleeping?

Gary Eighteen months now!

Bob They say it gets better.

Gary It can't get any worse. Do you want any eats?

Bob Not bothered.

Gary The Peterborough file, what shall we do with it?

Bob Send a copy to Grantham, make sure Tony has a copy, and get a distribution figure from Leeds. We need that before we can make any sense of the Carlisle figure. If there's a problem, ask Dennis, he deals with that side!

They freeze

Mick (*to the audience*) That's the sort of thing they say in that office. It doesn't mean shit to anyone else, but they think they're the dog's bollocks!

They animate

Gary Are you still on for five-a-side?

Bob You know me and football.

Gary The Parks and Gardens lads have got a team!

Bob Just keep them coming!

Gary Where is Dennis, by the way?

Bob He's taken early lunch. He sits down by the new Chinese and has a burger.

Gary On his own?

Bob You could always join him if you felt like it! Do you need me for anything else?

Gary Don't think so!

Bob I'd better let you go, then!

Bob spins and looks at his computer screen

Gary exits

Mick moves around the stage. Lights

Mick (*to the audience*) Come dinner time everybody else has pissed off for lunch, but not Bob, he insists on working through…

Lights. Bob is busy typing into the computer. A light picks him out

Bob Adult links. No, don't want that. Gang bang students? No. One-to-one live chat? That'll do! Yes, I want to watch live sex? "Yes, I want to have live inter-action with you. My name is Jerome, what would you like me to do to you? Explain it in great detail." (*He watches the screen, and reads it*) Dirty sod. "Yes, I would like to watch you put a banana up you. What would you like me to do?"

Music swells and fades. The Lights fade on Bob

   Bob takes the computer elements offstage with him, but leaves the table

Mick stays on stage

Lights

   During the following, Anabelle enters. She has a large box of odds and ends, and will start clearing out

Mick I bet the whole office are logging on to the internet just to see what's on. They reckon porn sites are the most visited. I bet it's an epidemic in that office! Dennis never really wanted to work there! He'd have been much happier staying on our estate in Doncaster and working for Land Reclamation! I reckon it was Anabelle who wanted them to flit. It wasn't good enough for them, she wanted their Jenny to go to a better school...
Anabelle Look at all this stuff! We've had some of this since we first moved. Nearly ten years old, some of it! If I get it all out of the bedroom, can you put some of it in the loft?
Dennis When?
Anabelle Well, any time!
Dennis Not now?
Anabelle Well, this weekend!
Dennis I was going to do the garage!
Anabelle Can't you do that later?
Dennis And the loft?
Anabelle You could try...
Dennis What about the fish pond?
Anabelle Leave the fish pond but do the guttering.
Dennis Anabelle?
Anabelle Just the front bit; well, you'll have to do the loft, you can't swing a cat in her bedroom.
Dennis I haven't done the garage for months, and we've got all those bottles!

Anabelle Well, just do as much as you can, I'll have my mum and dad here at one, and I haven't got out of the kitchen yet. Oh, and can you find those shears that my dad lent us, he keeps going on about them, you know what he's like.

Dennis They're not in the garage, I must have told him five times.

Anabelle Look at the time and I haven't even got the chicken in!

Dennis Is Jenny up?

Anabelle She's in the shower.

Dennis That'll only take her another hour, then!

Anabelle She's going to a fancy dress tonight.

Dennis And I'm picking her up, then, am I?

Anabelle She can get a taxi, but...

Dennis No, I'll do it...

Anabelle Just don't hassle her, that's what you do, you hassle people! Hassle, hassle!

Anabelle exits

Mick turns to the audience

Mick I bet Dennis is in a nice routine, though. Supermarket, car wash, a bit of DIY. You see a lot like him down here, they're just ordinary blokes looking for a bit of something different.

Jenny enters; she is played by the actress playing Natasha. She is dressed as a cliché schoolgirl

Jenny I'm wearing it, it's a laugh.

Dennis Jenny!

Jenny It's fancy dress!

Dennis But what are you supposed to be?

Jenny It's St Trinians.

Dennis Is that what it is?

Jenny I'm eighteen!

Dennis I know and look at you!

Jenny What?

Dennis Well!

Jenny Dad, lighten up a bit.

Dennis And when we come back, try and keep the noise down.

Jenny I'll try!

Dennis Well, that's all right, then.

Jenny Fine!

Dennis When you get to Kent you can make as much noise as you like, but with Mum's nerves being like they are...

Jenny And that's my fault?
Dennis Well, it's because you're going away!
Jenny Oh, you're just...
Dennis What?
Jenny Over-protective!
Dennis And that's wrong, is it?
Jenny Well, it's not healthy.
Dennis Jenny?
Jenny Father!
Dennis All I'm asking is for a little bit of consideration...
Jenny I suppose you'd prefer it if I didn't go?
Dennis I'm not saying that!
Jenny You'd rather I stayed here and rotted?
Dennis There is nothing wrong with staying here!
Jenny Except it's boring and anyone who makes it has to go away!
Dennis I don't want this at the moment, I've got enough on with your mother!
Jenny You know it's true!
Dennis I don't know why you feel that going all the way to Canterbury is going to solve things?
Jenny Just let me grow up, will you?
Dennis Why, what's so good about growing up?
Jenny The freedom!
Dennis Oh, yes, that's absolutely right!
Jenny You're both on at me all the time.
Dennis Look at what you look like?
Jenny On at me, on at me. I can't bear it! Talk about keeping me on a bloody chain.
Dennis Oh, come on.
Jenny I can never do what I want. I'm old enough to vote but I can't go to a fancy dress like I want, where am I living?

Jenny exits

Anabelle enters

Anabelle What's going on?
Dennis I can't talk to her.
Anabelle Dennis?
Dennis I just can't win with her.

A beat

Anabelle Let's not have another argument.

Dennis I can't get through! Good grief!

Anabelle Can you remember her as a little girl?

Dennis Oh, don't start all that again.

Anabelle The twenty-third of February, it was snowing.

Dennis And why does she have to smoke in the house?

Anabelle We had to go all the way to the hospital with the window down!

Dennis I don't want to be falling out with her all the time!

Anabelle You'd run out of de-icer. I told you to get some. You never listen to me, do you? I told you to get some. I was stuck in the back, can you remember? Freezing to death!

Dennis I mean, I worry about her!

Anabelle Wasn't she beautiful? She was absolutely gorgeous, Dennis, don't you think?

A beat

Dennis I mean, I know she's a woman, but...

Anabelle Oh, dear!

Dennis A bloody grown woman.

Anabelle Will she manage?

Dennis Well, she'll have to, won't she? She'll have to get a part-time job or something. It'll be good for her. Show her how the world works.

Anabelle She'll not be short of cash, will she?

Dennis Why shouldn't she be, we are?

Anabelle Well, you've got that bit saved, though.

Dennis It's for a rainy day.

Anabelle Dennis?

Dennis She'll have to get a job, that's what they have to do. I don't know what, work in McDonald's, anything. She'll have to get herself sorted, and what does she look like?

Anabelle Oh, don't hassle her, that's what you do...

Dennis I mean, I'm pleased she's done well, but she's cost us a bloody fortune.

Anabelle Well worth it, though.

Dennis Why she had to go to a private school is beyond me. I didn't go to a private school.

Anabelle I know that, love, look at you.

Anabelle exits

Dennis What is she wearing? Just what is she bloody wearing?

Lights. Music: Vivaldi's Mandolin Concerto in C Major

We are in a very upmarket restaurant. The table is now laid with knives and forks, a candle set, no plates

Bob and Gary in suits, they sit, with much hilarity in the air

Bob Well, that was nice, makes a change, don't you think, Dennis? I've brought Dee here a few times, she loves it.

Gary Nice and quiet anyway!

Bob He's looking for somewhere to get his head down.

Dennis Jenny didn't sleep for the first two years.

Gary Thank you, Dennis, that's very reassuring. Everyone else I've spoken to have said that theirs slept through. The whole thing is a conspiracy. I mean, nobody even told Sophie how painful the birth was going to be.

Bob How is Louise?

Gary She's all right really.

Bob What exactly is it?

Gary The specialist says it's an arthritic thing.

Bob Will she grow out of it?

Gary He reckons, but I tell you, bloody hard work.

Dennis Make the most of her, Gary, when they're leaving home, it's crucifying.

Gary It can't be worse than having no sleep, Dennis!

Bob You two are worse than the girls in the office!

Gary Sorry.

Dennis Yes, let's have some man's talk!

Bob Speaking of which; have you heard that we're having to slim down Chester? Tony told me that they'd had an audit done and the IT fella's told them they could lose six with the new on-line connections.

Dennis Hell fire!

Bob Losing six!

Gary What about us?

Bob Well, you never know, do you?

A mobile phone rings. Each of them reach for their phones. It is a real pantomime

Gary I think that's me!

Dennis I think it's me actually!

Bob It could be me, I'm waiting for...

Gary finds his phone

Gary No it's not me.

Dennis finds his phone

Dennis Typical, mine's switched off. I think the battery's faulty, to be honest!

Bob finds his phone and answers it

Bob Bob Lawrence. ... OK! ... OK, that's fine, and Marie, oh, that's all sorted, then, is it? ... What, all three, good! And don't forget to get the tickets, will you? ... You're on to it, OK, love, oh, and listen, don't let Jim Ballard see that letter yet, will you, I want to re-draft it before he does... OK? (*He puts the phone down*) I wonder about that girl!
Gary Didn't I see something about him in the paper?
Bob Who?
Gary Jim Ballard? Wasn't there something about him and some client?
Bob Oh that?
Gary Some sleaze thing?
Bob That could happen to any one of us!
Dennis There's no smoke without fire.
Bob Very possibly!
Gary Well, if it's not on Clapham Common, it's in the White House!
Dennis I'm bored with all that. It's every time you turn on the TV.
Bob Well, it sells, Dennis.
Dennis It may well do, but I don't want to know about who's doing what to who. They're all tarred with the same brush anyway.
Gary Fancy keeping a dress with semen stains on it?
Bob My mother said, you could tell she was dirty when she didn't wash her dress!
Gary If they're that intelligent, how come all these bloody ministers and politicians continually get caught with their pants down? It doesn't say much about their ability to run the world, does it? Half of them can't have a sly shag without getting caught.
Bob I think they want to get caught, it's part of the buzz!
Dennis It's all about getting your kicks, isn't it?
Bob It is and all, bloody queer, though, when you reckon it up!
Gary Bob gets his watching Leeds United.
Bob Now I know that sounds perverse, but there you go!
Gary You can get arrested for that, you know?
Bob Highly intelligent people have always had peculiar sexual tastes, didn't you know that?
Gary Really?
Bob That's what they reckon.
Dennis Speaking as one who didn't go to university, that could be true.

Gary It can't be that bad, Dennis?

Dennis I'm happy enough.

Gary There you go, then.

Dennis Frustrated, but...

Bob I mean, look at the Clinton job!

Dennis Oh, don't set me off on that!

Bob Well, he got away with it!

Gary But he didn't do anything.

Dennis No, that's absolutely right!

Gary Good on him! Anybody who can get a blow job while bombing Iraq gets my vote.

Dennis The world's going bloody mad!

Gary Did you read that about the Lord Chancellor, they had this vote or something about whether or not he should be able to stop wearing tights.

Bob I saw that!

Gary Yes, but half the silly sods in the Lords voted for him to keep wearing them!

Dennis Yes, they're all bloody perverts, that's why!

Gary You never know!

Bob Well, everything's on a spin.

Dennis I can just see it!

Bob I think we live in a much more open society, though.

Dennis Do you think we do?

Bob Course we do.

Dennis I think we only think we do!

Gary Steady, Dennis, you're losing me!

Dennis Compared to mainland Europe we're still behind.

Gary What do you think about the euro?

Dennis I don't follow it...

Bob They should have a referendum.

Gary Why, they know they'd lose, it's all about business.

Dennis Every time you turn on the telly, some bloke's got his pants down, or some twat's been caught ripping somebody off. I'm glad I'm a little minnow, I can tell you!

Gary It's the temptation, isn't it?

Bob Business is sexy, so they say.

Dennis No, it's men and women, Bob, we're pathetic?

Gary Speak for yourself, Dennis!

Bob Look at the French. The women there expect their men to have a mistress, there's something wrong with him if he hasn't got one!

Dennis Yes, but that means that all the women must be mistresses to some other bloke?

Gary So sort that one out!

Bob Well, it seems to work for them.
Dennis Well.
Bob Yes?
Gary Yes, well, I suppose it does!

A beat

Dennis Lucky sods!

A disingenuous laugh

Bob Well, we'd better...

They consult their watches

Gary Look at it...
Dennis Better get back.
Gary Just when it was getting interesting...
Dennis How much is the...?
Bob Oh, no, I'll get this...
Gary No, come on, Bob, let's split it...
Dennis Let's split the bill at least!
Bob No, I'll get this!
Gary Well, if I'd have known you were getting it, Bob, I would have had the rump steak.
Bob I know that.

Another laugh

No, I'll get this one, you can get one on Thursday!
Dennis Why, what's so special about Thursday, where are you going?
Bob Didn't Marie tell you?
Dennis No!
Bob She is going to have to go, that girl!
Gary We're booked in Thursday night.
Dennis Where?
Gary There's a weekend conference!
Bob Sorry, Dennis mate, I thought you knew?
Dennis Next Thursday?
Bob You are coming, Dennis, aren't you? Don't let me down, it's all bloody IT and high-tech. We need you!

Music: Ace of Base's All That She Wants. *Lights*

Bob and Gary exit, taking with them the restaurant settings

Anabelle enters with a load of washing

Lights. Music fades

Anabelle We discussed this when she went for interview. If she gets in, I'll take her, that's what you said.
Dennis What can I do?
Anabelle And now you just drop it on me!
Dennis It was dropped on me!
Anabelle You just drop it on me, "I'm going to Amsterdam"!
Dennis What can I say?
Anabelle Can't you get someone to go for you?
Dennis Yes, good idea, why don't you go?
Anabelle Don't be ridiculous!
Dennis Well, talk sense, how can I get somebody to go for me, honestly...?
Anabelle I'd take her myself if I could drive.
Dennis What can I say?
Anabelle Four months ago you agreed to this.
Dennis I know.
Anabelle Four months ago!
Dennis I've heard you!
Anabelle And now you're shouting.
Dennis I missed the away day in Scarborough last March because it was your Sophie's anniversary and we had to go down there. I missed the away day in Preston because you had a migraine, I can't afford to miss this. Good grief, do you think I want to go? The last thing I want to do next weekend is listen to Dick Van Dyke, or whoever the hell it is, rabbit on about computer locators and European logistics. I'd rather do the guttering, to be honest!
Anabelle I just can't believe you've let us down like you have!
Dennis I'll not go!!
Anabelle Oh, don't be daft, you've got to!
Dennis And when they're looking to make cuts, don't be surprised...
Anabelle Oh, we're off again, shout, shout, shout!
Dennis Shut up, will you, and listen to me for five bloody minutes...
Anabelle Shout, shout, shout, shout, shout!

Lights. Anabelle and Dennis freeze

Jenny enters and will speak to the audience

*When Dennis and Anabelle speak, they become animated, then they freeze
once more whilst Jenny continues*

Jenny It's not that they are real arguments! I could cope with real arguments!
Dennis Just shut up! Shut up!
Anabelle No, I won't!
Jenny It's the constant tit for tat, the bickering, the point scoring, the ripping
bits off, the chewing bits up, the weeping wounds, the burning flesh!
Dennis You'll bloody keep on, you will!
Anabelle Yes, I bloody will.
Dennis You never give it a rest.
Anabelle And neither do you!
Jenny It's the never reaching across, never touching. It's the never caring,
the never thinking, the never settling, never holding.
Dennis Christ, woman, you've not been near me for bloody years.
Anabelle Oh, don't start all that!
Dennis It's true.
Anabelle Don't start all that bloody nonsense.
Jenny It's not that they hate each other, it's just that they don't love each
other. They did, but they'll never find it; it's buried beneath the shit in the
loft, the bottles in the garage, or it's rotting between the leaves in the front
guttering!
Anabelle Do you think I'm interested in that?
Dennis I know you're not.
Anabelle You're pathetic.
Dennis I know that, love, you tell me every bloody day.
Anabelle Pathetic.
Dennis There we go again!
Jenny And the more time they spend together, the less they want to tell each
other how they feel.
Anabelle Shut up, you silly man, can't you see what you're doing?
Dennis Oh, it's me, is it, it's me!
Jenny If they were real arguments, it would have been easier. If he'd've hit
her, it would have somehow been kinder. Then the whole thing would have
finished years ago!

Music: Shy Guy by Diane King. Lights

*Jenny and Anabelle help set the next location. A hotel room is fashioned on
stage from the main set. Gary and Dennis have to share a room. A bedside
cabinet, a telephone, and a window create a bedroom. Neither man is happy
with their room sharing. Dennis stays down stage, looking out at Amsterdam
by night*

Lights. Music fades out

Gary Well, I didn't see it like this!
Dennis Nor me!
Gary Shall we get unpacked?
Dennis The last time I shared a room I was fifteen. I was on a Scout trip to Runswick Bay.
Gary Well, don't get any funny ideas.
Dennis We didn't get any sleep that night because one of the lads had brought a glossy magazine, and we had a masturbating competiton that lasted all weekend!
Gary Well, there's no change there, Dennis, we'll be having one of them later!
Dennis You might.
Gary Hey and don't be having a sly one while I'm in the loo!
Dennis Runswick Bay? Gor and we thought it was so exciting! We thought we were living!

Gary picks up a hotel What's On *magazine. He plays most of the scene reading the magazine*

I can't believe I'm sharing a room. I thought I'd have a jacuzzi and a sauna. I thought I'd have a nice quiet weekend just taking it steady. I'd even brought a book.
Gary Hey, listen to this!
Dennis What is it?
Gary *What's On in Amsterdam*!
Dennis And what is on?
Gary I don't know, I've not been reading that bit, I've just been reading this!
Dennis What?
Gary There's a whole list of escort services! There's pages of the stuff!
Dennis That should keep you busy, then!
Gary They come to your room and all! Two hundred guilders for an hour, it even gives the price. What's that, two hundred guilders?
Dennis Sixty-five quid.
Gary They'll come to your room for sixty quid?
Dennis Not this room, they won't!
Gary You just ring up.
Dennis Like ordering a take away! They come in a box on the back of a scooter!
Gary There must be twenty numbers here! Listen to this: Sexy Students, I fancy that. You know what students are like. I was at it all the time. Oh, look at this, it says, do not call during college hours!

Dennis Bloody hell!

Gary I might give them a ring.

Dennis What for?

Gary To see what's what?

Dennis Meaning?

Gary Well, get one over!

Dennis What for?

Gary Well...

Dennis What?

Gary Well, you know...

Dennis What?

Gary Don't you fancy one?

Dennis Do I bloody hell.

Gary It's in here.

Dennis I don't want one!

Gary You can have a "Dutch Student".

Dennis I don't want one.

Gary Are you sure?

Dennis Positive.

Gary I'm having one.

Dennis Well, I'm not.

Gary You can have a "Dream Escort", dining companions for him and her, or a "Sophisticated Lady".

Dennis I think I'll leave it!

Gary Well, I'm going to get one.

Dennis Are you serious?

Gary Yes, I might try one.

Dennis Why?

Gary Why not?

Dennis Well, what shall I do?

Gary I thought you didn't want one?

Dennis I don't...

Gary Get a Sophisticated Lady.

Dennis I don't bloody want one!

Gary Why not?

Dennis Because I've already got one.

Gary I bet you haven't got one that'll service you all over, though, have you?

Dennis How do you know?

Gary It's fantastic, man, they come, you go out for a meal, do all the chat and you know you're at least on for a shag at the end of it. Absolutely perfect.

Dennis And what about the cost of the meal? Is that all in? Waken up! It's sixty-five quid just to get them here; then a meal, and wine, a taxi! I mean,

you don't mean to tell me that a Sophisticated Lady is going to make do
with a Big Mac and some fries? I'm on a limited budget this weekend
anyway.

Gary You should try a student, then, they like burgers.

Dennis You're not going to phone one, are you?

Gary Why not?

Dennis Well, what shall I do?

Gary Well, I thought if you went out for a saunter, I could see what's what!

Dennis You're not serious, are you?

Gary Well, I mean, it's here, isn't it? It's what's in the magazine!

Dennis Let's have a look! (*He takes the paper*)

Gary Makes you wonder, Dennis!

Dennis No, it's all a load of rubbish, you don't want to be doing any of that.
Just be thankful for a good night's sleep.

Gary Well, there is that!

Dennis Bloody bizarre, isn't it?

Gary Do you think they're all for real?

Dennis I would have thought so!

Gary It makes you wonder.

Dennis Well, good luck to them, if they want to make a living jacking blokes
off, good for them! I don't think I could stomach it!

A beat

Gary So what time are we on tomorrow?

Dennis Half eight, Bob said. He's upset because he couldn't get tickets for
the Leeds/Ajax match. It was his little surprise. He played hell with Marie.
I thought he was going to have a fit!

Gary What's he doing now, do you know?

Dennis No idea, I notice he got a single room, though!

Gary Executive perks!

Dennis I hope you don't snore?

Gary I hope you don't fart!

Dennis Only when I snore!

A beat

Gary Bob'll be sending out for some of that, you know?

Dennis I wouldn't be at all surprised.

Gary Oh, ay, he's into all that. He's been to two conferences out here this
year already.

Dennis And I bet he didn't have to share!

Gary Marie told me that she saw him on the internet. He'd logged on to one of those sex line things. Apparently the screen was flashing up his credit card details. You can log on to somewhere out here and watch them having sex.

Dennis What's the point?

Gary Apparently you can tell them what to do. It's one of them inter-active jobs!

Dennis He's into all that, is he?

Gary They'll do anything for you, by all accounts.

Dennis Yes, but would they do my guttering?

Gary It'd cost you.

A beat

Have you ever tried one of those sex line things?

Dennis Eh?

Gary That phone sex stuff?

Dennis I wouldn't be able to handle it. I'd be all excited just thinking about ringing up!

Gary I rang one up last week.

Dennis Well, I hope you're not going to be ringing up tonight! That's all I bloody want. You heavy breathing down the phone all night.

Gary This bird says: "What have you got between your legs", so I says "A fish".

Dennis Well, whatever turns you on, Gary!

Gary Yes, it's good to talk.

Dennis Phone sex would be no good for me anyway.

Gary Why not?

Dennis Well, I'm going deaf in this ear for a start, and my phone hand's my wanking hand...

Gary stops Dennis

Gary Yes, yes, yes, all right. I know we're sharing a room, Dennis, but don't feel that you have to tell me everything!

A beat

Dennis I wonder what he'll want to do when the conference finishes?

Gary Well, he was on about going for an Indonesian. He told me that there are some places where they reckon you can have a blow job under the table!

Dennis Oh. I don't fancy that!

Gary Well, we could go and have a look. Mind you, if the head-waiter's got no teeth, let's give a body swerve and head to the pizza place!

A beat

Dennis Strange, all this!
Gary All what?
Dennis The way they sell sex.
Gary It's just different!
Dennis I think I'd feel a bit sorry for 'em.
Gary For who?
Dennis The girls who do it. They come to your room, you don't know them. Presumably there's some pathetic conversation and then it's down to business. It sounds like a bloody circus.
Gary I've always liked the circus.
Dennis Somebody's making a packet.
Gary We'll have to have a look down the Red Light District, though, won't we?
Dennis It's the biggest attraction according to that magazine.
Gary What time is it now?
Dennis A quarter to twelve!
Gary We could go down there now, I reckon it's still early.
Dennis You go if you want, I'm whacked. Anyway, we've got to get up early! I might watch a bit of a film and then call that it. (*He picks up a movie card*)
Gary What's on?
Dennis Let's have a look. *The Borrowers*.
Gary Seen it!
Dennis *The Full Monty*!
Gary Seen it!
Dennis The Adult Channel!
Gary What's on the Adult Channel?
Dennis Thursday night, let's have a look. Midnight? *I Will Suck You*!
Gary Oh, right.
Dennis Have you seen that?
Gary Not yet.
Dennis What's it about, do you think?
Gary I've no idea!
Dennis I'll go and run a bath. (*He makes for the exit*)
Gary What a disaster, Dennis, we're here in the sex capital of the world and all you want to do is wash your hair and have a bath. We ought to be out there seeing the sights, mate!

Lights

Anabelle enters

A light picks her out, she is arranging flowers in a vase. Gary and Dennis freeze. Lights

Anabelle Well, I don't really think about him, to be honest. I mean, we haven't got that much time, time for ourselves, time for time.
Dennis You go, if you're that keen!
Gary I might do!
Anabelle Time for little things; for being nice, for holding, for sharing, for caring.
Dennis You don't know what you dealing with, Gary.
Gary I've got a pretty good idea, Dennis!
Dennis It'll mess your head up.
Gary Get off, man!
Anabelle There's no time for quiet, time for alone. I think about making time, but there seems to be none. I've got the house, and the garden, and the pond, and with my mother getting on, I've got the fears, and the dread!
Dennis It's just a johnny down the bog, mate.
Gary It's more than that, man!
Dennis Is it bollocks!
Gary It's about being alive.
Anabelle I mean I love him and all that. But I just take him for granted. I take him for him! I know that sounds awful, sad, but we're a team, we're a unit, an outfit. He's just completely reliable. Just there beside me, part of me, a limb, an extra arm for the washing, just there to straighten the flowers, mow the lawn, hold the sheets! Just there like a suit, like a tie, just there like old brogues! He's just there, isn't he, he's just Dennis!

Music: horny, loud. Lights

Anabelle exits

Dennis, Bob and Gary animate; they are in the red right district for the first time. They gently saunter, chatting

Lights. Music fades under

Bob So what do you think to your first Indonesian, Gary?
Gary What the hell was it?
Dennis I enjoyed it.
Gary A bit bloody spicy, though.
Dennis A pity about the football, Bob!
Bob That bloody girl, you know she got tickets for the Arsenal game? How do you mistake Ajax for Arsenal, I ask you?

Dennis What did you make of all that this morning?
Bob I thought they could have sold it a bit more.
Gary Ay, that's right, Bob. That's what I thought.
Bob It's bloody long way to come to sit and listen to somebody drone on.
He should have put some life into it! I could have done better myself.

They stop and look around the space

Gary So is this it, then?
Bob No, it's not just here, it goes all the way down towards the Krasnopolsky
Hotel at that end, and back down to the old church.
Gary So what are we doing, then?
Dennis We can just have a look, you know, see how the other half live!
Gary We've got to go in, though.
Dennis You what?
Gary We've got to go into one of the sex shows!
Dennis You're joking, aren't you, it'll be a right rip-off.
Gary We've got to have a look.
Dennis You go and have a look.
Gary Oh, come on, Dennis, we can't come down here and not have a look.
Dennis Bloody hell, what's he like? He wanted a hotel visit last night. Now
he wants to get us murdered in one of these places.
Gary Give over, man. We've got to go in. What do you reckon, Bob? Have
you been in?
Bob I never have actually.
Gary And if you believe that, you'll believe anything.
Bob Well, I'm easy.
Gary Oh, come on, Dennis. You never know what you might see.
Dennis I could guess.
Bob And I dare say that you'll not be far wrong.
Gary Well, come on, guys, are we in or what? We look like tourists just stood
here, are we going in or what?

They both look at Dennis

Dennis Oh, come on, then!

Music: Lilly Was Here. *Lights*

*Gary, Dennis and Bob find a seat each and watch the live sex show, which
is taking place in the fourth wall. A spotlight highlights each of them*

Bob Well, you certainly get what you pay for!
Gary You do, you get live sex!

Dennis Would anyone like a mint?

Bob What?

Dennis Would anyone like a mint to suck on?

Bob Not for me.

Dennis Gary?

Gary Not at the moment, Dennis, thanks!

Dennis I don't mind sucking a mint, it helps me concentrate.

Bob That's right!

Dennis These are lovely these, I got them at the airport.

Gary I couldn't stomach anything at the moment.

Bob You what?

Gary I've got these bloody pains in my stomach.

Bob Well, there is it, Dennis. Served up on a bloody plate. Zena she's called.

Dennis It's like being at the bloody zoo!

Bob It's not what you get at home, is it?

Dennis I think it's utterly sexless!

Bob Well, they're doing their best, Dennis.

Gary I feel a bit off it!

Dennis What's wrong?

Gary I think I'm going to shit myself, to be honest!

Bob Well, nobody would notice in here.

Dennis In fact, if you got up on stage they might give you a few guilders for it!

Gary I think it must be that Indonesian, I've never been able to deal with spicy food.

Dennis We had a carpet like that, you know?

Bob Like what?

Dennis That! We had a sheepskin carpet just like that. I think Anabelle got it from what used to be Lewis's in Leeds.

Bob I don't know about you, but I'm not looking at the carpet, Dennis.

Dennis No, I know that, but it just caught my eye, do you know what I mean?

A mobile phone rings

Bob What's that?

Gary What?

Bob Somebody's brought their mobile.

Gary It's not me!

Dennis answers his phone

Dennis (*into the mobile*) Hallo!

Gary Dennis, man?

Bob is astonished by the show

Bob Oh, look at that!

Gary I feel bloody queasy, to be honest.

Dennis (*into the mobile*) Jenny? Have you got there?

Bob Oh, that's awful!

Dennis (*into the mobile*) What are the digs like? Does everyone seem OK?

Bob Oh dear!

Dennis (*into the mobile*) No, I'm just sat in my bedroom having a drink.

Bob Now that is sexy.

Dennis (*into the mobile*) No, I think there's a disco on, it's somebody's wedding, I think.

Bob Oh dear!

Dennis (*into the mobile*) Anyway, I'm glad you've got there. Listen, I'll have to let you go, love, there's someone at the door, room service. Give us a ring later, and we'll have a proper chat; watch what you're doing; don't do anything... (*The signal fades*) lost the signal. She's got there, so that's good anyway. One less thing to worry about. I was supposed to be taking her, but...

Bob Did you see that?

Dennis No? I was...

Bob Good show, don't you think?

Dennis They look bored to death.

Bob Oh, I don't know.

Gary I wonder how it's going to end?

Bob I could guess!

Music swells then fades under Tish's speech

The men all laugh. Lights. Dennis, Bob and Gary freeze

Tish, a prostitute in her late 30s, wearing very little, comes into a spotlight

The men only animate on their lines

Tish I do the live sex for two years! Rudi and me make the live sex every day. So it is OK, Rudi lives in my apartment, we have Lilly, she is three, so it is good, OK.

Bob Would you fancy it, Dennis?

Dennis I couldn't raise the interest, Bob.

The men laugh together

Tish We make good live sex; one o'clock, three o'clock, four o'clock. Maybe it's a little cold sometimes; and all faces looking...!

Gary I wonder what they're thinking about?
Dennis Haven't got a bloody clue!
Bob He's probably going through a shopping list.

The men laugh together

Tish We laugh afterwards, we wonder if maybe they have never make sex.
Bob Do you think he knows her?
Gary I should think he does now!

The men laugh and freeze

Tish So then, Rudi goes, I don't know why, he just go. OK? Like he has gone crazy, no me, no Lilly!
Bob He's making it last, Dennis!
Dennis There's no wonder if he's thinking about the bloody shopping!

The men laugh and freeze

Tish So I do not want to make live sex any longer. Hassan, he say you now do live sex with Jorgan with no condom; I say yes, I do live sex with Jorgan, but with condom, always with condom, with Rudi no condom. But Hassan say no condom, so I quit, I say fuck you arsehole, I say fuck you!

Black-out. Lights. Very loud rap music: One Night in Heaven *by M People. We see the brash neons of the Red Light District. Natasha, and Tish, now in her window, walk across the front of the audience, they encourage the audience to use them. Dennis, Bob, and Gary remain frozen. The girls walk threateningly across the front of the stage*

Natasha You like?
Tish Hiya, baby?
Natasha Hiya, OK, you enjoy?
Tish Hallo, baby?
Natasha Massage, you like massage? Hiya, I speak good English. I give you good time.
Tish Hallo, yes, please!
Natasha Hiya!
Tish Come, yes, please!
Natasha You like?
Tish OK, yes, please!

Music fades. Tish and Natasha make their way back to their windows as the men begin to animate

Dennis Oh dear!

Gary Yes, they're frying tonight.

Bob There you go, Dennis!

Dennis Bloody hell!

Tish Yes, please!

Natasha Yes, good time, you like?

Gary What do you think?

Dennis We're in hell.

Bob It's circus, isn't it?

Gary Yes, I've always liked the circus.

Dennis So have I, but I never liked the bloody clowns, though.

Natasha Yes, hallo, good time!

Tish I give you good time.

Gary I think you are in there, Dennis!

Dennis Bloody ridiculous!

Gary I think he's in!

Bob Well, if you can't pull down here, Dennis, you ought to hang yourself!

Dennis I don't want to pull.

Tish You like, German? You like?

Gary The young one's got her eye on you, Bob.

Tish You like, all three?

Dennis All three?

Gary What did she say, all three?

Dennis It's bad enough sharing a bloody room. Without any of that!

Natasha Hallo, we have fun?

Bob She's nice, don't you reckon?

Natasha Hallo!

Gary She's got all the bits!

Dennis Come on, let's keep walking.

Tish Hallo?

Dennis I think that one is bloody desperate!

Tish Hallo!

Gary Are you going in?

Dennis Me?

Gary Get in, man!

Dennis You what? It'd be like the slaughter of the innocents!

Tish Hallo, OK, yes!

Natasha Hallo baby!

Bob I think I've seen her before.

Gary You're joking!

Bob No, honest, she reminds me of somebody.

Dennis She wasn't on Blind Date, was she?

Gary Talk sense, man!

Dennis No, I'm serious!
Bob She might have been.

The men attempt to drift away

Dennis Don't keep looking at her, I think she's getting the wrong idea.
Natasha Hallo!
Dennis We're not stopping around here, are we?
Natasha Hallo, sexy baby!
Gary We're only window shopping, Dennis.
Dennis Ay, but she's only a bit of a kid, isn't she?
Tish Good time, nice big one?
Gary Go on, Bob, you've scored, mate...
Bob Do you think so?
Natasha Hallo!
Bob She's all right!
Gary I thought they might all be pigs, but...
Bob Very nice.

A beat

Gary You never been in, then?
Bob I've never had this much time before.

A beat

Dennis We're not just going to stand here all night, are we? (*He moves away*)
Gary What's up, Dennis, they won't bite?
Dennis I'm not so sure!
Natasha You like?
Bob What do you think, then, Dennis?
Dennis It's a lot different to trailing around B and Q with Anabelle.
Tish You like?
Bob Do you fancy it?
Gary I don't know.
Bob Chicken!
Gary I don't know if I've got the bottle!
Bob Bloody chicken, eh, Dennis?
Gary No, I'm just being honest.
Bob It's a bit up-front, isn't it?
Gary It's a bit real, do you know what I mean? I mean, they are just stood there selling sex, I just find the whole thing bloody bizarre.
Bob What about you, Dennis?

Dennis No, I've never liked second-hand shops.

Gary Hey, Dennis man, these girls are supposed to be clean, they have check-ups and everything.

Dennis Good for them.

Bob I thought that's why you wanted to come down here, Dennis?

Gary That's right!

Dennis Come off it.

Bob Isn't that what he said?

Gary Absolutely!

Dennis I didn't want to come down here, I was happy enough sitting in the bar. It was that maniac who wanted to look.

Gary You wanted to look as well.

Dennis Right, well, we've had a look, now let's get off!

Gary We've only just got here...

Bob Yes, fair enough, let's have a bit of the atmosphere.

Dennis Well, fair enough, but is...

A beat

Gary Do you reckon it's safe, then?

Bob Well, that's what they reckon. I don't know if I could perform, I usually need a few pints...

Gary Nice, though.

Tish You like, OK? I give you free titty show!

Dennis This one here is giving away freebies now!

Gary Get in there, Dennis!

Dennis Hey, listen, if anything's free, it's probably not worth having.

Bob Oh, I don't know.

Natasha Hallo, you like?

Bob Yes, I like.

Natasha You like good time?

Bob Well?

Natasha I give you real nice sexy time!

Tish Hallo!

Natasha You no like?

Bob I like very much.

Natasha Good.

Bob Very sexy.

Dennis Don't encourage them, man, for God's sake!

Natasha I give you real good time.

Tish You like, OK? OK, baby?

Gary How much is it?

Bob I don't know, I could ask?

Dennis Let's leave it and get off.
Bob (*to Natasha*) How much?
Natasha Fifty.
Bob Fifty guilders.
Gary How much is that, then?
Dennis Come on, let's leave it!
Gary How much is that, then, Dennis?
Dennis Bloody leave it.
Gary What's fifty guilders?
Dennis There's about three point two guilders to the pound?
Bob I got a bit more than that.
Dennis So that's about sixteen quid.
Gary Sixteen quid!
Bob Sixteen quid, well, that's not bad.
Dennis That's a rough "guess-timate".
Bob I'll just go and have a chat with her, you know, see what's what!
Dennis Let's leave it!
Gary Oh, man, he's in!
Dennis Bob, come on!

Bob moves towards Natasha

Tish Hallo!
Bob Hiya!
Natasha How are you?
Bob Me? Fine, how are you?
Natasha OK.
Bob So, erm, what's what?
Natasha You like?
Bob Well, yes...
Natasha You come?
Bob In there?
Natasha Sure.
Bob How much?
Natasha Sucky fuck?
Bob Sounds good.
Natasha Seventy-five guilders. You pay cash!
Bob No problem. (*He presses fifty guilders into Natasha's palm*)

Tish calls to Gary and Dennis who are surprised but excited

Tish Yes, you like too? Come good time?
Gary Oh, man!

Dennis Oh, hell!
Gary Oh, man!
Dennis Oh, shit.
Gary That's Bob.
Dennis I know.
Gary That's Bob Lawrence.
Dennis I know.
Gary Bang in there. Bob Lawrence, boring Bob. Bob the computer man!
You should see him playing five-a-side, he's a piece of wood and suddenly
he's in there!
Dennis Oh, hell!
Gary Oh, man!
Dennis Well, this is bloody ridiculous!
Tish Come you, yes, good time!
Dennis What can you say?
Tish Yes, baby!
Dennis Listen, as soon as he comes out we're getting off!
Gary Well, I...
Dennis As soon as he comes out!
Gary Oh, man!
Dennis The minute he comes out.
Gary Why?
Tish (*to Dennis*) You no like?
Dennis It's outrageous!
Tish (*to Dennis*) You no like?
Dennis Very nice.
Tish (*to Dennis*) You like?
Dennis No thanks, I've just eaten.
Gary Oh, man, it's exciting!
Dennis I'm not saying it's not.
Gary It's brilliant.
Dennis It's the atmosphere, though!
Gary It's brilliant down here.
Dennis That's the problem.
Gary Tempting, isn't it?
Dennis Of course it bloody is.
Gary There's no wonder it's a tourist attraction.

Tish is dancing to a disco song

Tish English?
Dennis Yes!
Tish Ah, English, bad fucks!

A beat

Gary Actually, love, I'm half Welsh, he's English!

Dennis Yes, and I know that, my wife's been telling me that for the last twenty years!

Tish Come, baby, you have a good time, I give you a massage, you like a massage?

Dennis I'm sure I would.

Gary Go on, Dennis, that sounds good!

Dennis You go in, then.

Tish You like massage?

Dennis Just ignore her.

Dennis and Gary attept to ignore Tish, but she works harder

Tish (*to Gary*) Hallo, you like massage?

Gary Here you are, Dennis, she's talking to you, don't be so ignorant, you'll give us a bad name in Europe!

Tish You like massage?

Dennis Yes, I like massage.

Tish I give very good massage, very long, no fucky fuck.

Gary That sounds just about right, go on!

Dennis Give up, man, once I'd got in there I'd probably never come out again!

Tish I give long massage.

Dennis She'd probably break my neck.

Gary I could do with a massage myself actually.

Dennis Well, there you go, get in there, just what you're looking for!

Tish (*to Dennis*) You no like?

Dennis Lovely!

Tish I give you good titty show!

Dennis Oh, she's off!

Tish You like titty show?

Dennis (*to Tish*) I like the Sooty show.

Tish Excuse me?

Gary Nice one, Dennis. The Sooty show. It's a puppet!

Tish Puppet?

Gary A bloke shoves his hand up its arse.

Tish Excuse me?

Gary I think we'd better forget that!

A beat

Dennis Listen, as soon as he comes out, right, let's clear off.

Tish I give good massage.
Gary Yes, I bet you do.

A beat

Dennis (*to Gary*) Are you listening, as soon as he comes out!
Tish (*to Dennis*) Hallo?
Gary You know what this means, don't you?
Dennis Yes, we're in hell!
Gary We're not!
Dennis Ay, it means he's bloody sex-mad.
Gary Well, there is that!
Dennis Well, what else, then?
Gary Well, we'll both have to have a go!
Dennis Why will we?
Gary Because we will!
Dennis You can!
Gary Course we will!
Dennis Give up!
Tish Hallo, baby!
Gary Oh, come on!
Dennis What?
Gary Well, he's gone in, hasn't he?
Dennis Like shit off a shovel!
Gary So what is he saying?
Dennis He's saying, "Look at me, I'm a sad bastard"!
Gary Don't you think he's opened the door for us?
Dennis No, I just think he's gone for a shag and we're stood here waiting for him.
Gary Yes, but look at the way he just ploughed in! He's thrown down the gauntlet!
Dennis Don't be so bloody soft!
Gary If we don't go in, he'll have got one over on us, you know what he's like!
Dennis Get away!
Tish I like, OK! I do you both, OK. Eighty guilders!
Gary He expects us to do the same!
Dennis Come on?
Gary Well, he's saying it's all right, isn't he?
Dennis I thought we'd just come for a look?
Gary Well, he's just raised the ante, hasn't he?
Dennis Not for me!
Tish I do two, OK, eighty guilders!

Dennis Oh, we're off again!

Tish Hallo!

Dennis She's doing a discount here now!

Tish You like two?

Gary What did she say?

Dennis She'll do us both for eighty guilders.

Gary Eight?

Dennis Eighty! Bloody eight, what do you think she is, a charity? Bloody eight guilders, what planet are you from?

Tish You like two?

Gary She'll do us both for eighty guilders? What's that, then?

Dennis Twenty-five quid!

Gary Twenty-five?

Tish We have nice good time!

Gary Twenty-five quid for two, that's not bad, is it?

Dennis Yes, it's reasonable, but it's not good business, is it?

Gary Listen, you can have anything you want, you know?

Dennis Well, I'm not having it with you.

Gary Why not?

Dennis Sharing a room is bad enough!

Gary Just think, man, this is one of the few places on earth where you can get just what you want!

Dennis Well, you get in there!

Gary You could live out your fantasies.

Dennis I couldn't.

Gary Just think about it.

Dennis I feel bloody sorry for them, to be honest!

Gary Sorry for 'em?

Dennis I think they look pathetic.

Gary Oh, ay, and you've got the perfect sex life, have you?

Tish Yes, please!

Dennis I'm not saying that.

Gary So you haven't?

Dennis Who has?

Gary You don't mean to tell me you wouldn't like a change now and again?

Dennis I don't even think about it, to be honest.

Gary Well...

Dennis What?

Gary There you are, then.

Tish You no like? (*She is, lost on Gary and Dennis. She sits for a while and smokes*)

Gary Come on, be honest with yourself. You don't mean to tell me that you and Anabelle are all over each other?

Dennis I've just said we're not, but that doesn't mean I'm going to run amok down here!

Gary You must fancy it, though?

Dennis Well, anybody would!

Gary You must think about it?

Dennis Not as often as you obviously do!

Gary It's just a shag.

Dennis I know what it is.

Gary The world won't slide into decay if you do it.

Dennis It would, if everybody did it!

Gary How do you know they're not doing it and you're the odd one out?

Dennis It wouldn't suprise me, I'll tell you that!

Gary These girls'll do anything!

Dennis I know that!

Gary Absolutely anything you want and they'll do it. These are the best in the world!

Dennis Well, go on, get in if you're that keen.

Gary I might.

Dennis Well, I'm not, I'm going to leave it and when he comes out I'll piss off and and get pissed up!

Gary Dennis, this is Amsterdam, if you don't get stoned and go in here they deport you! (*He begins to wander around the stage. He is contemplating going in with Tish*)

Tish You like, uh?

Gary Just thinking.

Tish You like?

Gary A massage maybe!

Tish I give good massage?

Gary Just thinking.

Tish You like massage?

Gary Could be!

Tish You come, we have good time. I give you nice good massage.

Gary OK!

Tish I massage you real good!

Gary Just the massage, how much?

Tish Massage?

Gary Massage, no fucky?

Tish I give good massage, thirty guilders!

Gary Thirty guilders, what's that, Dennis?

Dennis About a tenner!

Gary A tenner?

Dennis About!

Gary A massage a tenner, well that's not bad, is it?

Dennis It depends what she's massaging.

A beat

Gary Well, I'm in.
Dennis Right, then.

Gary makes his way towards Tish's window

Tish We have real good massage!
Gary See you later.
Tish I massage you real good time!
Gary Oh Dennis man, I've got to get in there. I love Amsterdam, don't you?

Gary exits

Dennis (*deadpan*) Oh, yes, it's absolutely fantastic!
Tish I do you next, OK, baby? You like fucky Tish? I do you next time!

Music: In Old Amsterdam *by Ronnie Hilton*

Lights as a delighted Gary enters the window. Tish closes the curtain on her window, and as the music plays, Dennis walks over to the window and peers inside

Fade to Black-out

ACT II

House Lights fade. Music under: I Just Want to be Loved *by Culture Club*

Mick is standing C

He takes up the mop and begins to mop the stage once again as we saw at the beginning of the play. He mops vigourously

Mick I never tell anybody what I do. Like it's not on my passport, do you know what I mean? I think we're very constipated when it comes to sex. They're very casual about it out here. It's right in your face out here. I tell you, I've seen that many porno films in this last year, that when I get into a lift with a woman, I expect her to go down on me. No, I do! It must have an effect, do you know what I mean? I mean to say, if you lock it away and pretend it doesn't exist, that's not right, and I don't know whether this is any better, to be honest! (*He mops more*) And it's all for men, isn't it? I mean, don't get me wrong, but what would it be like if all these windows had men stood in them? Eh? Can you imagine that? All stood there in their little white knickers, with their knobs in a pouch? I bet we wouldn't get as many down here then. Maybe we would. (*He mops more*) I don't know, but it makes me wonder about men. You see, I think men would actually shag somebody different every day, given half the chance! Most of the blokes I know want to have sex with every woman they meet. "Hallo, how are you? Nice to meet you! Right, knickers off, very nice! What were you going to say, more tea, vicar?" That's the beauty of Amsterdam, you can do that here! Yes, men are pretty pathetic when it comes to women, always have been, always will be, it's a universal given! (*He stops mopping*) Fucking hell, that's a mega thought, isn't it? What about that, me coming out with a mega thought? (*He puts on his Dennis costume*) When I saw Dennis stood out here, I was going to talk to him, I was going to have a little chat, but I wasn't sure what to say: I was going to say "All right, then, Dennis, how are you, mate? You won't remember me, but we used to live across the road at number thirty-eight, my mam did your ironing, when your wife had migraine. You looking for a shag, then?" But it's not the sort of thing you say, is it? So I just nodded, and he nodded back like suddenly he was Mr Sex Show and he knew all about what went off down here...

Gary comes from Tish's window. Tish herself comes and stands in her space

Gary Right, well, cheers for that!
Tish I see you OK?
Dennis All right, then?
Gary Yes, not bad.

A beat

Dennis He's still in there.
Gary Bloody hell, what's he having?

A beat

Dennis Not bad, then?
Gary Not bad...
Dennis Right!
Gary What do you want, Dennis, a full match report?
Tish Hallo.
Dennis I think she wants you back.
Gary No, it's you she's after.
Tish Hallo, you like sexy?
Dennis Have you heard this?
Gary (*to Tish*) He's got to wash his hair!
Dennis Don't encourage her!
Gary It's just a laugh.
Tish Hallo, you no like fucky?
Gary He does.
Dennis Leave it, man.
Gary He's a millionaire.
Tish OK to come!
Gary He's very rich he is.
Dennis Give it a miss.
Tish You no like?
Gary How long is he going to be?
Tish Hallo sexy, hallo English?
Dennis Look at her, man, bloody hell.
Gary Nice, man.
Dennis Well, not bad, but I don't want it ramming down my bloody throat!
Gary No comment.

Tish is trying to work her skills on them both

Tish Hallo!

Dennis I don't know about you, but I always liked a bit of romance.

Gary I mean, where do we live, just think about it. We can't even get a drink after eleven o'clock usually, unless you've got a signed passport and a blood sample from the Pope. We're living in the past.

Dennis You wouldn't want this at the bottom of your street, would you?

Gary It could be handy.

Dennis We're not ready for it, Gary. I mean, we've only just got used to Sunday shopping!

Gary There was a bloke at the conference who reckoned you could watch a Jap woman have a shit if you wanted.

Dennis Oh, please.

Gary No, straight up. I was going to try and have a look but with my stomach being a bit ropey I think I'll give it a body swerve.

Tish Hallo, please, good time!

Bob enters. Natasha comes to her window

Bob Oh, well!

Dennis Are we going to make a move now, then?

Gary All right?

Bob Not bad.

Dennis Oh, dear, man!

Bob What?

Dennis Well, I mean.

Natasha Hiya!

Gary Look out, she's ready for another one.

Dennis He's just been in here...

Gary Only for the massage.

Tish Hallo, please, sexy boy!

A beat

Gary Well, that's management for you. Straight in, no fannying about!

Bob What have I told you, business is war.

Gary Straight in!

Bob You two were stood thinking about it and there I was.

A false sense of relief

Gary Did you barter with her?

Bob Well, I asked her what's what?

Gary Took your time, though?

Bob Yes, well.

A beat

Gary I wonder how much they make a night?
Dennis Well, ten massages is a hundred quid.
Gary And what will they do, six nights a week? Man, we're talking serious cash here. Let's say a shag is fifty quid.
Dennis Which it's not.
Gary And they do ten shags a night, that's five hundred quid. Six nights week, that's three thousand quid.
Tish Hallo!
Natasha Hiya!
Tish Hallo, please!
Gary We're in the wrong job, Dennis.
Dennis Have you only just noticed.
Bob No wonder they look so smug.
Gary But what do they spend it on?
Dennis Well, it's not underwear, is it?

A laugh lightens the tension

Bob So shall we have a few beers?
Gary Well, why don't we split up for a bit?
Dennis What for?
Gary Well, you know, let's just have a sniff about on our own for a bit. I mean, I think we look like a Social Services outing shuffling about in a group. Why don't we have half an hour going solo and meet back here, I need to have a slash anyway and get some smokes.
Bob Well, I'm sorted, so whatever!
Gary Are you into that, Dennis?
Dennis Well, I mean?
Gary So what, shall I see you back here in half an hour? And be careful, Dennis, don't get lost.
Dennis I wouldn't be suprised, you know what my sense of direction's like.
Bob I bet he's straight back down to that live show, aren't you?
Dennis Oh, ay, that's right. I might even get on stage and join in.
Bob Now I would pay good money to see that.
Gary I wouldn't.
Bob Why not?
Gary It sounds bloody obscene to me!
Dennis Ay, it would do!
Gary Now don't you go and get bloody lost, Dennis, we don't want to have to take you home in a body bag.

Dennis You go where you want, I'm going to have a float about around here and get some souvenirs.

Lights. The three men stand in spotlights. They are cruising the red light district

Gary Out on my own, I feel a lot better!
Bob Now I can do what I really want!
Mick In a video cabinet, they sit and watch endless porn...
Gary Two hundred and fifty channels of filth...
Bob In goes another ten guilders...
Mick And they laugh like it's nothing out of the ordinary...

All laugh

Bob And in goes another ten guilders...
Gary Two hundred and fifty channels of endless, storyless shagging...
Mick And they laugh like it's having no effect...

All laugh

Gary Two hundred and fifty channels on two screens in stereo...
Bob With recliner seats, and a neat little bin...
Mick And the mop man, mops and mops and mops...

All laugh

Gary And out into the night...
Bob And into another club...
Mick A revolving bed...
Gary A girl gyrates...
Bob You watch through a letter box...
Mick Endless, mindless, friendless sex ... sex, sex, sex!
Bob It's fantastic!

All laugh

Gary And out into the night...
Bob Past whore after whore...
Mick Hundreds and thousands of drifting men...
Gary Hands in pockets...
Bob Smirking, prowling; caught in a trap...
Mick Like shoppers in Harrods they search for a bargain...

All laugh

Bob It's fantastic.

Lights

The three men exit as the two prostitues come from their windows and make their way down to the audience

Natasha You like sexy.
Tish Good time?
Natasha Hiya, sexy, you like Bob Marley?
Tish Hi, baby, good time?
Natasha You like Bob Marley, baby?
Tish Hallo, sexy!
Natasha Hi, you like Madonna?
Tish Hallo, sexy.
Natasha You like Lighthouse Family, hallo ... guut band, uh?
Tish Hallo, sexy baby!

Natasha turns to Tish as she wanders upstage. Showing her her new nail varnish

Natasha Which you like best, blue or green?
Tish For you?
Natasha Blue or green?
Tish For you blue.
Natasha I like blue.
Tish Sure, blue looks good. (*To the audience*) Hallo, hallo, baby!

The girls make their way back to their windows as Bob enters. He now has a Leeds scarf around his neck. He looks at Natasha

Natasha Bob Marley!
Bob Bob Marley, great!
Natasha Good band...
Bob Absolutely.

Gary enters, smoking

Gary No Dennis, then?
Bob Not yet.
Gary I knew he'd get fucking lost.

Bob Where've you been?
Gary Just about? You know, having a sniff. You?
Bob Just had a beer, waiting for the footy to come on.
Gary I thought you might have had another look.
Bob Naa ... seen one, you've seen them all.
Gary That's right!
Bob Busy innit?
Gary It's bloody madness on the next street. I've been talking to a group of lads from Leeds, they've been through four already.
Bob Bloody hell!
Gary Oh, ay, they come out here once a month, and go through a dozen before they go back.
Bob Well, we need to get in front of a telly, it's on Dutch TV, there's a pub near the bridge.

Dennis enters, carrying a plastic carrier bag

Gary Here he is, look!
Bob We thought you'd been abducted, Dennis.
Dennis Have you been down there, you can't move!
Gary You been back in, then, Dennis!
Dennis Not me! Have you?
Bob No chance.
Dennis Well, I've got myself sorted anyway. I managed to get most of the stuff I was after.
Gary That's good, then!
Dennis Anabelle wanted me to get some clogs for her sister, so... (*He reveals some large clogs*)
Gary (*genuinely*) Oh, yes, they're nice.
Dennis They're not bad, are they? And I got her a T-shirt as well. Most of them had cannabis leaves on, I'll get her some flowers, but she just wanted me to get some authentic Dutch stuff.
Gary Take her a dildo back, Dennis.
Dennis I can't see that going down so well. What do you reckon to this? (*He reveals a Motorhead T-shirt*)
Gary I'm not so sure.
Dennis No, I know what you'mean, but it was all they had. I mean, I could have got her one with two rhinos mating, but I don't think she'd've appreciated that.
Gary Whereas I bet she loves that!
Dennis I'll get her some stuff from the duty free.
Natasha Hiya!
Tish Hallo, English ... hallo.

Natasha Hallo, Bob Marley OK...

Dennis repacks his carrier bag

Gary Bob Marley, what's she on about?
Bob I'll say this much for them, they never tire, do they?
Dennis It's not real, though, is it?
Gary It is, Dennis.
Dennis I'm sure it is, but...
Gary Yes, it's definitely real, I can vouch for that!

The penny drops with Dennis

Dennis Oh, no!
Gary What?
Dennis Bloody hell...
Gary What?
Dennis Not you and all?
Gary There's some lads from Leeds who have had four already.
Dennis Well, whatever...
Gary Hey, Dennis, these twats'll do anything!
Dennis Whatever lights your fire, Gary.
Bob All right, was it?
Gary Well, my legs were a bit wobbly, but...
Dennis Where was this, then?
Gary Back there? Excellent, man, I went for the French and all!
Dennis Oh, no...
Gary Well, Bill Clinton reckons it's not sex, so...
Bob Listen to him?
Gary No, you think about it. The most powerful man in the world reckons it's not sex, so that's OK by me, no guilt, you see. In the mouth isn't sex, it's official.
Bob He's got a point.
Dennis Awful!
Gary Pity I don't smoke cigars, I could have done the full Monica! You think about it. Clinton's sent the message out; stick it in their gob and it's not sex, now man, what can you say, he must know what he's talking about because he's got his finger on the button.
Dennis Well, if you believe that you're as thick as pig shit!
Gary I'm not saying I believe it, I'm saying that's the message. You take it up with Bill and Hillary, they know what it's all about, Dennis.
Dennis I knew he'd have to go in.
Gary I tell you something, I could stay down here all night, feel about ten years younger.

Dennis Well, you don't look it, the stress has put years on you.

Gary I feel it, though. I wish I'd gone for something else now.

Dennis Never bloody satisfied, is he?

Gary I wish I'd gone for something a bit different.

Bob It's funny, isn't it, because the moment you come out you want to go back in again.

Gary I wish I'd've had the Russian, now I think about it.

Dennis What the hell's that?

Gary Tit job.

Bob So are we calling that it?

Gary He's Leeds mad, Bob, I'm asking you, what would you rather watch, eleven blokes in shorts or this lot?

Bob I know, but I never miss a game.

Gary Aren't you up for another?

Bob No, I want to get to a telly.

Gary They haven't got a chance against Ajax.

Tish Hallo, hallo, Gary?

Dennis You didn't tell her your real name, did you?

Gary What is it, Dennis, a secret? I told her your name and all, and where you live!

Natasha Hiya, OK, OK?

Gary Well, listen, I can't stay down here just watching this.

Dennis No, right, let's make a move, shall we?

Gary I'm going again.

Dennis Eh?

Gary Dennis, it's only twenty quid a pop, you can't get a round of drinks for that back home. And listen, I'm not having sex, am I?

Dennis Come on, let's go back!

Gary I'm not going back, I'm going in!

Dennis Bloody forget it, man, let's go back and go to bed!

Gary Oh, that's it, then, Dennis is out.

Dennis I'll see you back at the hotel.

Bob Hang on, Dennis, I'll come with you. We can nip and watch the game!

They make to move

Gary Wow, hang on, guys! Wait for me to do the business, it's only fair, surely?

Dennis No, I'm going to get off!

Gary Dennis, hang on, if you drift about down here, you'll probably end up down a back alley somewhere with a needle up your arse. Listen, wait for me, I'll be ten minutes and then we'll all go and watch the footy!

Bob If I miss this match I'll swing for you.

Gary I'm going in, aren't I? (*He walks towards Natasha*)

Tish springs into action

Tish Gary, hallo, Gary, I love you real good, uh!
Gary Maybe later.

Gary disappears in with Natasha

Tish Hallo, yes, this time, hallo this time. Why you no come? OK, good sexy?
Dennis Sorry.
Tish You no like sexy?
Dennis Well...
Tish Maybe later, uh?

A beat. Tish retires to her seat

Dennis This is not really on, is it?
Bob Well, you get off, Dennis, if you want. If you walk to the end, and do a left you're back near the Central station. It's only ten minutes.

A beat

Dennis She's only a bit of a lass, isn't she?
Bob Most of them are.
Dennis I dunno, Bob.
Bob Yes, how the world works, Dennis.
Dennis Bloody hell.
Bob She told me that the blokes who had been in before me just wanted to watch her sit on a dildo and sing.
Dennis You what?
Bob That's what she said. Just watch her sit on a dildo.
Dennis And sing?
Bob And sing!
Dennis Bloody hell.
Bob Dear me!

A beat

Dennis What did she sing, did she say?
Bob *No Woman No Cry*!
Dennis Bloody hell!

Bob *No Woman No Cry*!

A beat

Dennis I never really got into Bob Marley.
Bob Nor me.
Dennis Jenny liked Meat Loaf for a time, but...
Bob *No Woman No Cry.*
Dennis Bloody Bob Marley, eh, Jesus!

Tish has stirred

Tish You come, OK? Yes, please, it's OK, I will love you all night!

A beat

Dennis If you want to go again, I mean, you know?
Bob Do they scare you, Dennis?
Dennis Not as much as Anabelle would if she found out I'd been hanging
    about down here! She's a bit starchy when it comes to all this.
Tish You like fucky fuck?

Dennis and Bob can't quite connect. The conversation is strained

Dennis She works for the Lifeboat Appeal, you know?
Tish Hallo, good time fucky?
Dennis She's a lovely woman in her way.
Bob Well, she seems nice from what little I've seen.
Tish Hallo, yes, nice time!
Bob You've got to give her some credit, haven't you?

Gary comes from Natasha's widow

Gary Well, anyway, there you go!
Dennis That was short and sweet!
Gary You said it.
Bob Right, let's get off, then.
Tish For you, hallo, good time, you like titties?
Gary Why don't you get in there, Dennis, you know you want to!
Dennis Give over!
Bob Leave him, he says he's not bothered.
Gary Fair enough. We don't want to set him off with an angina attack or
    something!

Dennis I'll tell you something, ten years ago I'd've been the first to get in there!

Gary Oh, here we go.

Dennis I would.

Gary Well, go on, then, get in, in fact, I'll pay for you! (*He digs into his wallet*) Come on, let's get you sorted. Does she take Blockbuster video cards? (*To Tish*) Do you take AA cards?

Tish Hallo, Gary, yes, please!

Dennis Don't be pathetic.

Tish Yes, I like. Hallo, hallo! OK, stuff you, OK. Stuff your arse!

A beat. Tension

Tish exits. Her window is empty

Gary So what are you saying, that I'm pathetic?

Dennis Well...

Gary Hey?

Dennis Well...

Gary Hey?

Dennis No, I'm not saying that.

Gary Yes!

Dennis I'm not saying that you're pathetic.

Gary Yes you are.

Dennis I'm saying I'm pathetic.

Gary Well, you are, Dennis.

Bob Leave it, let's get off!

Gary I'm not trying to force him. I just know that he'll go away on Sunday night with some clogs and a shitty load of tulip bulbs, wondering what it would have been like.

Dennis Yes, that's right!

Gary What is your life, Dennis?

Dennis You what?

Gary Tucked up in bed at half-past nine with Anabelle in a hairnet? It must be about as enticing as burying your mother!

Bob Hey hey hey, come on, leave it!

Gary There are men twice your age going with her.

Dennis So what?

Gary Treat yourself, no-one'll ever know about it!

Dennis No!

Gary I mean these girls don't save their dresses, you know? They're not going to suddenly turn up in Hessle and spill the beans.

Dennis I don't want to.

Gary Liar, everybody wants to, but some have the guts to do it!
Bob Just leave him!
Gary Leave him, he's a bloody arsehole.
Dennis I'm an arsehole and you've a little girl who can hardly walk and you're playing these tricks.
Gary Yes, I am.
Dennis Yes, you are.

A beat

Sorry for saying that.

A beat

Gary Look, get in there.
Natasha Hallo.

A beat

Gary I tell you what, I'll come with you if you want?
Dennis I couldn't think of anything more horrible!
Natasha You like, hallo, you like.
Bob Are we going to get off?
Natasha You come, yes, you come and we share a lovely moment! Hallo, you like good time. Come, yes. Oh, you no like?
Gary Oh, look at her, man.
Natasha Hallo, you share good moment?
Gary Just try it.
Dennis I thought we were going?
Gary I can't believe that he doesn't want to have a go!
Bob Right, we're off.

Bob makes to move but Dennis remains

Gary Look at him, he's dying to go in.
Dennis Am I?
Bob I thought we were going?
Dennis I don't know, to be honest!
Bob Look, let's either get you in there, or piss off and watch the footy.
Dennis I don't know, I mean, what do you say?
Bob What?
Dennis What do you say?
Bob Nothing.

Gary That's the beauty of it, go in there, tell her you want it in her mouth or
up her arse or something!

Dennis No, I'd better leave it.

Bob Right, come on, then!

Dennis Do you think I should, though?

Bob This is insane, make a decision!

Gary Do you want to know why I did it?

Dennis No!

Bob Are you going in or what?

Natasha Hallo, you like, I make real good fucky!

Bob Look, lads, this is important.

Gary I did it for me, that's why I did it.

Bob Good for you, let's leg it!

Natasha Hallo, you come, it's OK.

Dennis Oh, hell!

Gary Get in there, Dennis, Dennis, Dennis!

Dennis Pack it in, man, everybody's looking.

Gary Go on, go for it!

Dennis Oh, fuck it, come on, then! Somebody hold my clogs!

Bob Oh, Dennis man, don't be bloody long!

Dennis I won't, I won't.

Gary Well done, D!

Dennis Arghhhh! Look at me!

Gary Hey, man, put the T-shirt on, she might think you're Lemmy from
Motorhead!

Dennis No, I'm right.

Gary Turn your mobile off, you don't want it going off half-way through.
If it does, she might think you're bionic!

Bob Are we going to watch this bloody football or what?

Gary Five minutes, man, that's all it'll take him.

Dennis turns off his mobile and walks up to Natasha. Bob and Gary watch

Natasha You like?

Dennis You speak English?

Natasha Good English? You like for good time?

Dennis Yes.

Natasha You like fucky sucky?

Dennis What ever's going, love!

Natasha Seventy-five guilders, with condom.

Dennis searches out his money. He is nervous and struggles with his wallet

Dennis Whatever!

Natasha Relax, OK. You let Natasha show you what to do!

Dennis and Natasha freeze. Gary and Bob animate downstage

Gary I knew he'd have to do it.
Bob I just hope he's not long.
Gary He's got a dicky heart, hasn't he?
Bob Angina!
Gary Wait till they hear back in the office that we got Dennis in with one.
Bob I hope he doesn't die on us!
Gary Yes, that could be a bit awkward. Mind you, he'll probably not do anything?
Bob You reckon.
Gary I reckon a load of blokes get in there and can't perform. He's probably sat there in the nick telling her some story about Anabelle's piles! Either that or he's asking her where she got her carpet from. "Did you get that carpet from what used to be Lewis's in Leeds?"

Music: Just a Matter of Time *by Urban Species*

Gary and Bob laugh and freeze. A Light picks out Dennis. Natasha dances provocatively, as the scene progresses, she dances more and more raunchily

Dennis (*to the audience*) I could just imagine him in there. Not knowing which way to turn, the room spinning, the smallness, the heat, the tiled floor, the wet wipes, the smell of her!
Gary (*shouting to the window*) Go on, Dennis!
Dennis (*to the audience*) The neon, the feelings, the guilt, the lust, the smell of her, every inch of her!
Gary Go on, Dennis!
Dennis (*to the audience*) He is completely lost in there, for five whole minutes his mind is a blank. Jenny is lost, Anabelle has gone. I could see him inside her, holding her, pumping against her, fighting for his breath, sweat standing out on his forehead, his nylon shirt stuck to his back, his brogues slipping on the wet wipes, the tiled floor giving no purchase! I could see him looking around, taking in the room, noticing dust in the corners, chips on the emulsion, Anabelle wouldn't have stood for that. He sees a postcard from abroad, jeans folded neatly over a chair, a pair of trainers covered in mud, he sees two cassettes, Bob Marley and Enya. Jenny likes Enya! I bet wherever he looked he saw things that brought him back, brought him back from where he was!

A spotlight reveals Anabelle

Anabelle Dennis, can you take that rubbish from the garage to the tip for me, love?

Dennis (*to the audience; animatedly*) Yes, love, no problem!

Anabelle And don't forget to drop that stuff off at the bottle bank.

Dennis (*to the audience*) I won't be a minute, Anabelle!

Anabelle And when you come back, can you try and get all that dog mess from the bottom of my slippers?

Dennis Yes, love, I'll scrape it all off for you, don't worry!

Anabelle I did ask you to clear it up last week. I don't know why they have to deposit in our garden? There's a right dollop of it by the fish pond. I mean, I did try to clean it with a dish cloth, but quite honestly I got the damn stuff all over my fingers!

Anabelle exits

Lights. A musical climax, Natasha's dancing cools down. Dennis comes downstage. Sound fades. Silence. Dennis is very slow and silent as he comes downstage. Gary and Bob animate

Gary All right?

Bob Took your time, didn't you? They'll be kicked off by now!

Dennis I was as quick as I could be.

Gary That must be a world record, you've been in there nearly an hour.

Dennis Have I hell!

Gary Just over six minutes...

Dennis Oh, hell!

Gary Not bad, though.

Dennis Oh, hell!

Gary Well done, you did it!

Dennis Oh, don't!

Gary You did it!

Dennis Oh, dear!

Gary You did do it, didn't you?

Dennis Oh, yes, I did it, I'm sure about that.

Gary Well, there you are, then.

Bob Well, that's all right, then, can we now go and watch the bastard footy?

Dennis I need a bloody drink.

Gary It's your round and all, Dennis.

Bob Come on you, Leeds!!

Gary, Dennis and Bob exit

Natasha comes from her window. She slowly lights a cigarette and smokes

Natasha Hallo! You like Lighthouse Family, uh? (*She patrols around the stage*) Hallo, sexy time?

As she stands, Tish comes out and down stage. They both play the audience as punters passing

Tish Hallo!
Natasha Hallo, sexy?
Tish Hallo, sexy, hallo, you like?
Natasha Hallo?
Tish I work all night and not one single dick. Not one!
Natasha (*to the audience*) Hiya!
Tish So maybe I go home, and watch MTV. Maybe I go to bed tonight, uh?
Natasha No dick?
Tish One massage, thirty guilders. Crazy, very bad for me!
Natasha Hallo, baby!
Tish I'm not so hot tonight!

Natasha goes back upstage. Tish buttonholes a member of the audience

OK, you like? You like sucky fucky? What is wrong? You no like? Too like your wife maybe, go back to her tired tits, arsehole! Get out of here, what you come for, eh? You come to look, ja? You like to look, uh? Too scared to try; just to look, uh? Maybe you have one already? I fuck you real good time, ja, all positions! Too short, ugh, too tall, ugh? Too fat, too thin, too what? Too old? Too old maybe. Fuck you! OK? Fuck you! What do you think, too old, ja, I want the money, OK? I want the money! I give good fucky fuck, I want good money!

Music: Getting Jiggy With It *by Will Smith. Lights*

Tish storms back to her window and exits

Bob, Dennis and Gary bring on a bar and three bar stools, they are in a pub watching the football, in the fourth wall

Lights

Bob Smithy, what are you playing at? Come on!
Gary There's no structure!
Bob Come on, Leeds, there's only fifteen minutes left.
Dennis What's the score, nil nil still?
Bob One nil.

Dennis One nil?
Bob One nil, Dennis, Ajax scored five minutes ago!

The men watch TV

All Oooooh!
Bob Come on, Leeds!
Gary Good night, eh, Dennis?
Bob (*to the TV*) Hit it! Bowyer, have a go!
Dennis I was shaking like a bloody leaf when I got in there.
Bob (*to Gary*) He should have had a crack!
Dennis She was ever so nice, she could see that I was nervous.
Bob (*to the TV*) Oooh, well, pass, then, you pillock!
Gary He'll be having a whip-round for her in a minute.
Dennis Hey, not a word, right?
Gary Absolutely!
Bob (*to the TV*) Well, look at that, they're playing like ... have a go ...
    oooooh! (*He is anxious about the match, he is in a real sweat*)
Gary You all right?
Bob Did you see that?
Gary Sounds like you're losing it...
Bob Have you seen this? Dutch bastards!
Gary Calm down, man, the bar's full of Ajax supporters!
Bob (*to the TV*) Look at that.

A beat. As they watch the match

Gary So what did you go for, then, Dennis?
Dennis Oh, just, you know, nothing fancy.
Bob (*to the TV*) Offside, referee!
Dennis Just, you know?
Bob (*to the TV*) Corner! Bring 'em up, then!
Dennis What did you?
Gary Oh, I can't tell you that, Dennis!

All react to the TV

All Ooooohhh!!
Bob Nice shot, Bowyer, hard lines, lad.
Gary It was good, though!
Bob (*to the TV*) Oh, hell?
Gary What?
Bob He just brought him down from behind!

Dennis Free kick!

All watch the screen. The ball is struck, but goes low over the bar

All Yeees! Oooooohhh, bastard!
Bob (*to the TV*) It's supposed to go in the net, you useless shite!
Gary They'll not hear you!
Dennis They might if he shouts that loud.

A beat

Gary So what about you, Bob?
Bob (*to the TV*) Square ball, square ball! Nice ball. (*To Gary*) What did you say?
Gary What did you go for?
Bob I'm not telling you.
Gary Why not?
Bob Because I'm not.
Gary Oh, right, pulling rank just when we're getting down to detail.
Bob No. (*To the TV*) Cross it, oooh!
Gary The mouth?
Bob (*to the TV*) Goal kick.
Gary Come on, Bob, I want to know the sexual preferences of senior management. I want to know if they'll keep me on when the crunch comes.
Bob (*to the TV*) Goal kick! (*To Gary*) I'm not telling you.
Gary Oh, touchy.
Bob (*to the TV*) Hit it, have a crack! They've got to have a crack from anywhere!
Gary Tell us.
Bob No.
Gary Oh, stick it, then.
Bob (*to the TV*) Corner, surely.
Gary Tell us what happened.
Bob That was easily a corner!
Gary Come on, Bobby!
Bob Hey, just remember who you're talking to.
Gary Yes, an arsehole who won't spill the beans!
Bob (*to the TV*) Shoot, then!
Gary What's up, couldn't you manage it?
Dennis (*to the TV*) Offside that?
Bob You what?
Gary I thought it took you a long time.
Bob A mile offside.

Gary What's up, could you manage it?
Dennis That was offside!
Bob (*to Gary*) Careful, Gary!
Gary You what?
Bob I said careful, that is a big statement.
Gary Oh right!
Bob That is a large statement!
Gary Large statement, what are you talking about?
Dennis (*to the TV*) Ooooh, off the crossbar, did you see that?
Gary I was only asking a simple question.
Dennis (*to the TV*) They've no chance now!
Bob Just forget it, all right.
Gary All right, all right!
Dennis (*to Bob*) Oooh! Just off the crossbar!
Gary There's no need to have a fit!
Dennis (*to the TV*) Only a minute left.
Bob Why are you interested anyway?
Gary I was just asking.
Bob Oh, right.
Gary I was actually having a laugh!
Bob Fair enough.
Dennis Looks like they've had it, Bob.
Bob Yes, I know that, Dennis, that's bloody obvious!
Gary So what happened, then, are you going to tell us or not?

A beat

Bob Nothing.
Gary Oh yes, nice one!
Bob Straight up!
Gary Get off.
Bob You asked me!
Gary Nothing happened?
Bob (*to the TV*) Look at that! Full time!
Dennis I thought you'd been with her, though, Bob?
Bob Yes, I did...
Dennis So what went off, then?
Bob Nothing.

A beat

Dennis You what?
Bob I didn't do anything.

Dennis How do you mean?

Bob I got in there and I realized that I'd made a mistake. I was all up for it, but...

Gary He's pissing us about, it's a wind-up!

Bob No, we just sat and talked for a bit.

Gary You sat and talked for a bit?

Bob Yes, then after twenty minutes I came out. That's what happened!

Gary What did you talk about?

Bob Hey?

Gary What did you talk about?

Bob I don't know, anything, Amsterdam, the weather, the Lighthouse Family, Bob Marley!

Gary Oh, nice one, I put it up her back end, and he was just sat there discussing the weather and Bob Marley! How fucking civilised!

Bob What's the problem?

Gary What's the problem?

Dennis What's the problem? I've just shafted a lass no older than my daughter!

Bob Hey, steady!

Dennis Well, I mean to say...!

Bob laughs

Bob Don't blame me!

Dennis He thinks this is funny.

Bob Dennis?

Dennis Bollocks!

Bob Come on?

Dennis Bollocks!

Bob Dennis?

Dennis You could have told us this before.

Bob I did think about it, but I thought I'd lie like everybody else. But since you've pushed me...!

Dennis Well, fuck me!

Bob No, thank you, Dennis!

Gary He thinks this is funny!

Bob You did what you wanted.

Dennis Bollocks!

Gary So why didn't you?

Bob I don't know, it just seemed so bloody ridiculous. I went in, she asked me what I wanted; then she started to get on the bed thing, and I thought this is all wrong. So I bunged her seventy guilders and we sat and had a chat.

Gary A chat?

Bob That's all!
Gary A chat??
Bob Yes!
Gary What did you think it was, *Woman's Hour*?
Bob Piss off!
Gary A sodding chat?
Dennis I only did it because of you two bastards!
Bob I couldn't get past the fact that I didn't know her.
Gary Why, what did you want to do, take her out for a meal? "Come on, love, leave what you're doing, I'll take you to meet my family."
Dennis Bastards!
Gary "This is Natasha, she's a Czech whore, this is my mam, this is my dad, do you like Arctic Roll? Right, that's the introductions over, get up stairs and get your knickers off!"
Bob I was all revved up to do it, but something just gave way!
Gary Yes, your nerve!
Bob I dunno what it was, but it suddenly struck me that I couldn't go with somebody who didn't want to go with me.
Dennis But she did want to shag you, though!
Bob I mean, where's the romance?
Gary Well, listen to Catherine Cookson!
Dennis Bastards!
Bob And when she told me about these blokes from Essex, well, that just about did it for me!
Dennis This is just...
Bob She told me that they'd been back five nights in a row, and each time they asked her to do something more humiliating, because they could, and because she would.
Dennis Oh dear!
Bob I mean, at the bottom line, it's got to be mutual, hasn't it?
Gary Has it?
Bob Well, I don't know about you, but I've still got some self respect!
Gary Have you?
Bob I'd rather have a wank over the internet, if you must know!
Gary Ay, we know you would, it's all round the bloody office, mate. We know what you're up to every dinner time.
Bob Well, it is safer.
Gary That's not what they reckon, they reckon internet porn is perverting the nation's youth.
Dennis Yes, there's no wonder fewer people are watching telly!
Bob It's better than the real thing.
Gary How would you know?
Dennis So that's all you did, then, you just talked about music for twenty minutes?

Gary What the hell is there to say about Bob Marley that would take twenty
minutes?

Dennis I don't know, Bob, bloody hell, mate, bloody hell!

Bob What can I say, what could I do? Go straight in and come back out again?
What would you have said to that?

Dennis I thought he was up to all sorts, I was stood out here freezing my
bloody knackers off.

Gary Yes, while we were freezing to death, Bob was in there telling her about
his Cliff Richard collection, and she was telling him about all the charity
work she does. She's expecting the Nobel Peace Prize next year!

Dennis Bollocks!

Silence

Bob Well, I'm going to make some tracks, anybody want to come?

Silence

Dennis No.

Gary I'm staying put!

Bob Please yourselves!

Gary I might go back and shag her again!

Bob Good idea.

Gary Yes, I might go back and give her one for you, Bob.

Bob That'd be nice!

Gary Right up her arse!

Bob That's the best place for you!

Silence

Gary Bloody management, no contact with real people.

Bob One nil, eh?

Bob exits

Gary and Dennis sit. Silence

Dennis Bollocks!

Gary The man's an arsehole.

Dennis That's right!

Gary An absolute tosser!

Dennis Absolutely right!

A beat

Gary Well, you suprised me, Dennis. I didn't think you'd do it.
Dennis Well, there you go!
Gary Oh, hell, what a thought, you and her!
Dennis Bloody Anabelle, man!
Gary Oh, don't.
Dennis That bloody woman.
Gary That's right, Dennis, blame somebody else!
Dennis What does she expect me to do? Put my sex life in the loft with the rest of the stuff we don't want?
Gary I haven't got a clue!
Dennis Shall I take it to the bottle bank and bin it?
Gary I don't know, Dennis.
Dennis I love her, you know?
Gary Oh, leave it!
Dennis It's just not getting any better. There's nothing there! Nothing between us!
Gary Bob Lawrence? What an arsehole!
Dennis Oh, dear, Gary lad!
Gary What an arse, honestly.

A beat

Dennis I've had my fair share, you know.
Gary I don't need to know this, Dennis.
Dennis I've had an affair six years ago!
Gary No, D, leave it, mate!
Dennis I couldn't bloody help it. Anabelle never knew. She was a big woman and all, a lot older than me. Nice, but full, you know what I mean?
Gary Don't, Dennis!
Dennis Attractive! I mean, don't get me wrong, she was a real looker, oh dear! When she used to laugh, she used to frighten me to death, I thought she was going to swallow me! Goor, she was bloody funny was Kate! Worked for a solicitors' firm in town. We used to be at it all the bloody time! She was all over me.
Gary Oh, hell!
Dennis I felt so alive, I felt like I'd got a point, I felt so attractive.
Gary Oh, shit, man!
Dennis Yeah, can you imagine that; me feeling sexy? I felt like that when I was in there, I felt so bloody powerful! I felt so bloody alive, my heart racing, my legs, goor you should've seen me, talk about shaking in anticipation.
Gary Oh, shit, Dennis.
Dennis We shouldn't have to keep it in, should we?

Gary We didn't!

Dennis I talked to my dad about all this, years ago. He told me it never goes away, it keeps racing through your veins, always there, always pumping.

Gary Oh, hell!

Dennis Oh, yes!

Gary How old was he, then?

Dennis Seventy-nine!

A beat

Gary Sounds like a good bloke.

A beat. Gary begins to feel the remorse

Dennis I don't suppose you'll tell Sophie?

Gary Well, I might go and phone her right now!

Dennis What do they say, "To err is human, to forgive divine"!

A beat

Gary Well, what have we done, man?

Dennis No guilt, you said!

Gary That's right.

Dennis Look at Clinton?

Gary Sod Clinton. I've got a little girl, for God's sake.

Dennis So has he!

Gary (*stifling the humour*) Oh, don't, man!

Dennis Oh, come on, we've got to live, haven't we? It's like going to see the Eiffel Tower and not going up it, in a way!

Gary Dennis?

Dennis Well, it is. Anyway, it's only a one-off!

Gary I wish it was.

Dennis Eh?

A beat

Gary I said, I wish it was.

Dennis Oh, right.

Gary When Sophie had just had Louise I went into Hull. I don't know why. I'd just seen my daughter being born, and I drove around in a daze. I pulled up at these traffic lights, and a girl got in!

Dennis Oh, right!

Gary I didn't even stop to think about it. It was so exciting.

Dennis Oh, hell!

Gary I never used anything.

Dennis Oh, right!

Gary Funny, isn't it? I mean, it seems to be the right thing to do when you're here, but can you imagine how we'll feel when we're back in Princess Quay shopping?

Dennis Give up!

Gary I feel like we've been to the bloody moon! And I mean, what about Aids?

Dennis Oh, don't!

Gary I mean, I'm not religious, but it makes you wonder why it's developed, doesn't it? I mean, it's like the most natural impulse we've got and there's this big dark fucking shadow saying, naughty naughty!

Dennis Gary, you can go and watch a donkey and three jockeys have sex across there, don't start all this!

Gary We're not made right, are we? We've got all these drives and desires and nowhere for them to go! What a bloody mess, man.

Dennis Have another drink!

Gary I mean, you should've seen me at college. I went bloody mad.

Dennis Oh, don't start going on about students!

Gary I must have had a different bird every week.

Dennis Ay, I missed out on all of that!

A beat

Gary Your Jenny's at Kent, isn't she?

Dennis Doing law.

Gary Done well, then!

Dennis She's got a massive loan to pay back, I don't know how she's going to manage day to day, to be honest.

Gary A lot of them do phone sex, don't they?

Dennis Do they?

Gary Some mates I knew used to do it.

Dennis Oh, right!

Gary Hey, it's good money, D!

Dennis Bloody hell!

Gary I got a grant, but they have to take all sorts of work just to get by.

Dennis Well, Jenny's got her head screwed on!

Gary Funny thing about students. I saw this article in the *Mail on Sunday*. It said that instead of moaning about poor fees they should go and work in brothels!

Dennis Thatcher's got a lot to answer for.

Silence

Gary So shall we get off? If I stay here any longer I think I'll weep. What have we done, man. I could scream, oh hell, Dennis, man, what have we done? Shit! Soph? Sophie, oh, hell.

Dennis Oh, shut up and have another drink!

Gary But what have we been doing, eh, Dennis, what have we been bloody up to?

Dennis Don't worry about it, Gary, go home, go to bed, have a wank and don't say a bloody word!

Music: The Sweetest Thing *by U2. Lights*

The pub set is struck by a dancing Natasha and Tish

Tish and Natasha exit

Gary and Dennis exit

Lights. Music fades under

Bob enters. He is on his mobile. It is much colder than before

Bob (*into the mobile*) It's me! Everything all right? ... No, I'm fine; usual bollocks, but apart from that. ... Lost, yes I know, Bowyer came close. ... No, just a couple of beers... Listen, you're breaking up, love. I'm going to have to let you...

Dennis enters from Tish's window, he has his carrier bag and a bunch of tulips with him

Tish OK, ja, good, ja?

Dennis Fine!

Tish You here tomorrow?

Dennis Don't worry, darling, I'm here all weekend.

Tish You come tomorrow?

Dennis I'll be back, to get you sorted, love! Don't worry about it.

Tish We have real good time, Dennis, OK?

Dennis No problems, don't worry about it!

Tish We have a real nice time!

Dennis I might have a saunter and then...

Tish I see you later...

Dennis I'll be back, you needn't worry about that!

Tish walks back into her window

Bob enters

Dennis notices Bob. The two men stand silently looking at each other

Just, er...
Bob Yes, right.
Dennis Where've you been?
Bob Just drifting about.
Dennis Window shopping?
Bob That's about it!
Dennis Gary's gone back. He was getting a bit tired... So...
Bob Is he all right?
Dennis Yeah, yeah, he's fine. Getting a bit homesick, but...
Bob He's only a bit of a kid.
Dennis Nice bloke!

A beat

She's nice.
Bob Yes?
Dennis You should try her.
Bob Yeah?
Dennis Easy.
Bob Right!
Dennis No pressure. Good English and all!
Bob Yes?
Dennis Better than mine.

A beat. Tish pulls her curtain across and goes inside

Yes, she speaks good English. Right arse on her and all!

A beat

Bob It is just so...
Dennis What?
Bob Bloody odd, isn't it?
Dennis I love it!
Bob Yes?
Dennis No, I'm serious.
Bob Whatever!
Dennis Don't you fancy...
Bob No...

Dennis Well, I'm telling you...
Bob What?
Dennis She'll do whatever...
Bob Pointless, though!
Dennis Sommat to wank about, when I get back!
Bob Yeah?

A beat

Dennis No, she's good, this one... I mean, so was the other one, I mean, I
   bet they all are, but she just takes her time and you're sorted. And she'll do
   whatever ... you know?
Bob That's good, then.

A beat

Dennis So, didn't you want?
Bob In my head! I was all up for it, but haven't got the guts, Dennis.
Dennis It's not that...
Bob Didn't want to be compared, you know what I mean?
Dennis Compared?
Bob With every other fucker! Too much respect.
Dennis For her?
Bob For myself!
Dennis I'm just not thinking about it!
Bob It's a bit too surreal for me, you know what I mean? Nothing happening
   between us, just a load of bollocks that she'd obviously said a million times
   over.
Dennis I switched off.
Bob I couldn't...
Dennis Oh, I could. I've given myself the weekend off. Left my conscience
   in the room safe!
Bob I ought to batter your brains in, Dennis!
Dennis Why?
Bob You can't see the joke, can you?
Dennis What joke?
Bob It's in their eyes, mate. The lies in their eyes.
Dennis I didn't look in their eyes, Bob.
Bob They're just tarts dressed up as tarts, that's the joke!
Dennis You reckon?
Bob How are you going to live with it, Dennis? There's no going back, mate,
   you've crossed the rubicon!
Dennis Well, thanks for the lecture, Bob, I'd better let you go.

A beat. Bob moves to go and then he begins to laugh

Bob You know, I think it's funny, to be honest...

Dennis It is, it's fucking hilarious, Bob, that's why I'm off in for another and you couldn't get it up.

Bob Whatever...

Dennis Couldn't get it up, eh, Bob? Wait while we tell them all in the office! There you are, wanking yourself blind over the internet, but when it comes down to it you can't handle the real thing!

Bob So what?

Dennis Not go down so well with the five-a-side lads!

Bob I'll bloody eat you in a minute, you scabby little shit!

Dennis Could you, though, Bob?

Bob What?

Dennis Could you eat me?

Bob You're an arsehole, mate.

Dennis I know.

Bob An arsehole!

Kev enters from inside the sex club

Kev All right fellas? Live sex show? Sucky show, mate?

Bob No thanks.

Kev Good show!

Bob Not for me, I've got to wash my hair...

Bob drifts off stage

Kev and Dennis stand in silence

Kev What about you?

Dennis I've seen it.

Kev Good show, isn't it?

Dennis I thought the ending was a bit predictable!

Kev Have you seen the candle show? That's a good show!

Dennis Has Natasha had enough?

Kev You what?

Dennis Has she gone home?

Kev She's having a shower!

Dennis Right.

Kev The football's just turned out.

Dennis Eh?

Kev The match has finished, they'll be thousands down here tonight. She should make a packet. Every time Ajax play, it's bedlam!

Dennis And the English are always the worst?

Kev No, not really, you should see the Italians, they're mad for it! She'll be dead on her feet come four o'clock.

Dennis Oh, right!

Kev You fancy her, then?

Dennis You know how it is, once you get started!

Kev I wouldn't fuck 'em with yours.

Dennis I wouldn't let you!

Kev I see how many go in.

Dennis Yes, but I'm an arsehole.

Kev Yes?

Dennis Oh, yes!

Kev Yeah, we get a lot of arseholes down here.

Natasha appears at the window. She is wearing a different outfit

Natasha Hiya, sexy boy!

Kev There you go, man!

Natasha You come, eh … we have good time.

Kev Go on, man, give her one for me…!

Natasha walks off stage, while Kev crosses and exits

Lights

Dennis is stopped in his tracks by the arrival of Anabelle, and we have flashed back to the first scene

Anabelle I thought you'd got lost!

Dennis Delayed two hours.

Anabelle Have you had a good time?

Dennis I had a bit of a struggle getting everything you wanted.

Anabelle Well, you needn't have bothered.

Dennis Well, you said you wanted something getting, so…

Anabelle No problem with the flowers?

Dennis That was the easy bit.

Anabelle They have such beautiful flowers, don't they?

Dennis And I managed to get some bulbs as well, there's a bulb market, I thought I'd get some. And I've got some of that new perfume, Issey-something. They were going mad for it at the airport…

Anabelle Oh Dennis?

Dennis What's wrong?

Anabelle Well, it's the first time you've been away and actually brought me anything back!

Dennis It's not!

Anabelle Usually I'm lucky if I get a box of Quality Street.

Dennis Well, it's not everyday I get a chance to.

Anabelle But it's daft, we're strapped for cash as it is...

Dennis Well, if I can't get you a bit of something...

Anabelle I'm not complaining, I'm just saying...

Dennis I can't do right, for doing wrong!

Anabelle Did Jenny ring you? I told her to!

Dennis No, no, she rang, we had a right good chat. She seems fine.

Anabelle Well, at least she rang you... Well, I'd better get these into some water. They're lovely, aren't they? (*She moves to peck Dennis*)

Dennis I was thinking, you know...

Anabelle What, love?

Dennis She's a long way away, isn't she? I mean it's a three-hour drive, isn't it? I mean, what if she needs us?

Anabelle Let her grow up, you said!

Dennis I know, but, I mean, you never know, do you?

Anabelle She'll be all right, once she gets herself a little part-time job.

Dennis Yes, but what kind of work is she going to get?

Anabelle She'll get what there is?

Dennis I was wondering if we should help her out!

Anabelle With what?

Dennis Well, if she's strapped for cash. I mean I don't want her having to do some shitty menial job if she doesn't have to, do you?

Anabelle Well, no, but...

Dennis I mean, they end up doing all sorts. Gary was telling me. I thought if we dipped into that nest egg, it wouldn't really hurt, would it?

Anabelle I thought you were saving it for a rainy day?

Dennis Well, I mean...

Anabelle Well, she'll love that, won't she?

Dennis I mean, you never know, do you?

Anabelle Are you all right, Dennis, love?

Dennis Me?

Anabelle You seem a bit...

Dennis No, no, I'm fine, I've just had time to think about things, that's all. I'm glad to be home to tell you the truth. It's a funny old place, Amsterdam.

Anabelle Did you see the sights?

Dennis Well, we had a look, you know, but, nothing out of the ordinary, we didn't have much time, to be honest!

Anabelle Well, you can get on with doing the rest of the garage now.

Dennis That's right.

Anabelle That should keep you busy.

Dennis Absolutely.

Anabelle I dont know … conferences, eh? What a nuisance! I'll make you a coffee, shall I? (*She makes a move to exit*)
Dennis I think I might go away again, you get great treatment when you get back!
Anabelle Just let me know in advance next time.
Dennis Well, they reckon there's another one in Hamburg next month, so…
Anabelle You're not serious?
Dennis That's what he reckons.
Anabelle They won't want you to go again, will they?
Dennis Well, I…?
Anabelle Would you go?
Dennis Well, I'd have no option, would I?
Anabelle Oh, Dennis, Hamburg? Can I come?
Dennis I wouldn't have thought so.
Anabelle Oh, it's not fair, you have all the fun.
Dennis Fun? Is that what it is?
Anabelle Anyway, I suppose there is a good side to it!
Dennis What's that, then?
Anabelle I get good presents when you come back, so it's not too bad, is it?

Anabelle exits

A beat

Dennis No, you're right there, Anabelle, it's not too bad, is it?

Music: C U When U Get There *by Coolio*

Natasha enters her window and proceeds to dance to the music on her headphones

Tom and Kev enter, they have brollies against the drizzle

Mick disrobes his Dennis apparel and picks up his mop and bucket. He commences mopping

Tom Live show, sexy live show, come and see the sexy candle show, here you are, lads, sexy show, come on, what are you waiting for?

Kev enters

Kev Live show!
Tom Red hot live sex show. Come on, what's wrong with you?

Kev (*to the audience*) Hey, you been to the match? Come on, guys?
Tom Who's been playing?
Kev (*to the audience*) Come on, fellas, real sexy show!
Tom Who's on, then?
Kev Marga?
Tom That student!
Kev That's her.
Tom A bloody law student and she's doing this!
Kev She's got to earn a crust!

A beat

Tom So what does she do, then?
Kev Go and have a look if you're that interested.
Tom Is it a candle act?
Kev Go and have a look.
Tom I think they're rubbish, you know what's going to happen!

A beat

Kev You know, I can't believe that you took a les back to your apartment
    and you talked about art! I can't believe that you'd go for a les!
Tom We had a good chat!
Kev I just can't get over it.
Tom She was a nice lass.
Kev I just can't fathom it!
Tom She wasn't a les.
Kev She does a les show!
Tom She does a lesbo show, but she's not a les. It's an act. It's a show, it's
    a what's it? It's like all this bloody lot, it's an illusion.
Kev A bloody les!

A beat

Tom She any good, then, this student or what?
Kev Not bad.
Tom Oh, right!
Kev For a student!
Tom I might pop and have a quick look in a minute.
Kev I thought you said it was pointless?
Tom I might pop and have a quick squint.
Kev I thought you said it was all shite?
Tom I might go and have a shifty!

Kev Yes?
Tom Just a peep!
Kev Why?
Tom Well, everybody does, don't they? Everybody likes to just have a look!

Mick comes downstage

Mick You know, when I think about it, I don't know if it was Dennis Ashby that I saw. I see that many going in with the girls down here, all the faces blend into one! And when you're stoned as a bastard, they all look the same. I mean, when I think about it, it's all a haze! I'm not even sure that the bloke I saw was English. He could have been from anywhere, he could have been anybody! I mean, he could have been you.
Tom Live show.
Kev Live show.

Mick proceeds to sweep up. Tom and Kev hawk

Tish appears in her window

Tish Hiya, Mickey, you like good time?
Natasha Mick, yes! Come, you like, uh?
Mick Yes, OK, maybe later, OK?
Tom Live show!
Kev Sexy show!
Tom Live non-stop twenty-four hour sexy show!

The Lights fade as the Red Light Zone goes on and on and on. Music: Millennium by Robbie Williams. Mick mops more absurdly than earlier, Tom and Kev twirl their brollies. It is all going mad

Fade to Black-out

FURNITURE AND PROPERTY LIST

Further dressing may be added at the director's discretion

ACT I

On stage: Mobile bucket
Mop
Raincoat
Glasses
Bedside cabinet. *On it*: telephone
What's On magazine
Movie card

Off stage: Bunch of tulips, carrier bag full of souvenirs (**SM**)
Computer table, computer (**Bob**)
Large box of odds and sods (**Anabelle**)
Knives, forks, candle set (**SM**)
Load of washing (**Anabelle**)
Flowers in vase (**Anabelle**)

Personal: **Gary**: mobile phone, wrist-watch
Mick: mobile phone, wrist-watch
Bob: mobile phone, wrist-watch

ACT II

On stage: As before

Off stage: Plastic carrier bag, large clogs, Motorhead T-shirt (**Mick**)
Bar, 3 bar stools (**Bob, Mick, Gary**)
Umbrella (**Tom**)
Umbrella (**Kev**)

Personal: **Bob**: Leeds scarf
Gary: wallet
Mick: mobile phone

Mick: wallet containing money
Natasha: lighter, cigarettes
Bob: mobile phone
Mick: carrier bag, bunch of tulips
Natasha: headphones

LIGHTING PLOT

Property fittings required: nil
1 mixed setting. The same throughout

ACT I

To open: Overall general lighting

Cue 1   Music fades   (Page 5)
Change lighting

Cue 2   Boyce's *Symphony No. 4 in F Major* plays   (Page 6)
Change lighting

Cue 3   **Mick** moves around the stage   (Page 7)
Change lighting

Cue 4   **Mick**: "…he insists on working through…"   (Page 7)
Change lighting, spotlight on **Bob**

Cue 5   Music swells and fades   (Page 8)
Fade lights on **Bob**

Cue 6   **Bob** exits   (Page 8)
Change lighting

Cue 7   **Mick**: "Just what is she bloody wearing?"   (Page 11)
Change lighting

Cue 8   Ace of Base's *All That She Wants* plays   (Page 15)
Change lighting

Cue 9   **Anabelle** enters   (Page 16)
Change lighting

Cue 10   **Anabelle**: "Shout, shout, shout, shout, shout!"   (Page 16)
Change lighting

Cue 11	*Shy Guy* by Diane King plays *Change lighting*	(Page 17)
Cue 12	Hotel room is set *Amsterdam by night lighting through window; change overall lighting*	(Page 17)
Cue 13	**Gary**: "...out there seeing the sights, mate!" *Change lighting*	(Page 22)
Cue 14	**Anabelle** enters *Bring up light on* **Anabelle**	(Page 22)
Cue 15	**Gary** and **Mick** freeze *Change lighting*	(Page 23)
Cue 16	Loud, horny music plays *Change lighting*	(Page 23)
Cue 17	**Mick**, **Bob** and **Gary** saunter, chatting *Change lighting*	(Page 23)
Cue 18	*Lilly Was Here* plays *Change lighting*	(Page 24)
Cue 19	**Gary**, **Mick** and **Bob** sit down *Spotlights on each of them*	(Page 24)
Cue 20	**The men** laugh *Change lighting*	(Page 26)
Cue 21	**Tish** enters *Spotlight on* **Tish**	(Page 26)
Cue 22	**Tish**: "...I say fuck you!" *Black-out, then bring lights up, including brash neons of the Red Light District seen through window*	(Page 27)
Cue 23	**Gary** enters window *Change lighting*	(Page 37)
Cue 24	**Dennis** peers inside window *Fade to Black-out*	(Page 37)

ACT II

To open: Overall general lighting

Cue 25   **Mick**: "...around here and get some souvenirs."   (Page 42)
            Change lighting; spotlights on the men

Cue 26   **Bob**: "It's fantastic."   (Page 43)
            Change lighting

Cue 27   **Gary** and **Bob** laugh and freeze   (Page 52)
            Bring up light on **Mick**

Cue 28   **Mick**: "...brought him back from where he was!"   (Page 52)
            Spotlight on **Anabelle**

Cue 29   **Anabelle** exits   (Page 53)
            Change lighting

Cue 30   *Getting Jiggy With It* by Will Smith plays   (Page 54)
            Change lighting

Cue 31   **Bob, Mick** and **Gary** watch TV   (Page 54)
            Change lighting

Cue 32   *The Sweetest Thing* by U2 plays   (Page 64)
            Change lighting

Cue 33   **Gary** and **Mick** exit   (Page 64)
            Change lighting

Cue 34   **Natasha** and **Kev** exit   (Page 68)
            Change lighting

Cue 35   **Tom**: "Live non-stop twenty-four hour sexy show!"   (Page 72)
            Slowly fade lights to Black-out

EFFECTS PLOT

ACT I

Cue 1	To open *Music: Joan Osborne's* One of Us	(Page 1)
Cue 2	**Mick** starts mopping *Fade music*	(Page 1)
Cue 3	**Mick**: "…full of shit souvenirs in the other…" *Music:* Knocking on Heaven's Door *by Ladysmith Black*	(Page 5)
Cue 4	**Anabelle** enters *Fade music*	(Page 5)
Cue 5	**Mick**: "…they'd like to cut each other's throats!" *Music: Boyce's* Symphony No. 4 in F Major	(Page 6)
Cue 6	**Bob**: "…What would you like me to do?" *Increase music, then fade*	(Page 8)
Cue 7	Lights change *Music: Vivaldi's* Mandolin Concerto in C Major	(Page 11)
Cue 8	**Bob**: "Well, you never know, do you?" *Mobile phone rings*	(Page 12)
Cue 9	**Bob**: "We need you!" *Music: Ace of Base's* All That She Wants	(Page 15)
Cue 10	Lights change *Fade music*	(Page 16)
Cue 11	**Jenny**: "…would have finished years ago!" *Music:* Shy Guy *by Diane King*	(Page 17)
Cue 12	Lights change *Fade music*	(Page 18)

Cue 13   **Anabelle**: "…he's just Dennis!"   (Page 23)
Music: horny, loud

Cue 14   Lights change   (Page 23)
Fade music

Cue 15   **Mick**: "Oh, come on, then!"   (Page 24)
Music: Lilly Was Here

Cue 16   **Mick**: "…do you know what I mean?"   (Page 25)
Mobile phone rings

Cue 17   **Bob**: "I could guess!"   (Page 26)
Increase music, then fade under Tish's speech

Cue 18   Lights change   (Page 27)
Very loud music: One Night in Heaven *by M People*

Cue 19   **Tish**: "OK, yes, please!"   (Page 27)
Fade music

Cue 20   **Tish**: "I do you next time!"   (Page 37)
Music: In Old Amsterdam *by Ronnie Hilton*

ACT II

Cue 21   To open   (Page 38)
Music under: I Just Want to be Loved *by Culture Club*

Cue 22   **Gary**: "…what used to be Lewis's in Leeds?"   (Page 52)
Music: Just a Matter of Time *by Urban Species*

Cue 23   Lights change   (Page 53)
Musical climax, then fade

Cue 24   **Tish**: "…I want good money!"   (Page 54)
Music: Getting Jiggy With It *by Will Smith*

Cue 25   **Mick**: "…have a wank and don't say a bloody word!"   (Page 64)
Music: The Sweetest Thing *by U2*

Cue 26   Lights change   (Page 64)
Fade music

Cue 27   **Mick**: "…it's not too bad, is it?"   (Page 70)
             Music: C U When U Get There *by Coolio*

Cue 28   Lights start to fade   (Page 72)
             Music: Millennium *by Robbie Williams*

www.ingramcontent.com/pod-product-compliance
Lightning Source LLC
LaVergne TN
LVHW051756080426
835511LV00018B/3333